THE NATURE AND ORIGIN
OF THE
NEW TESTAMENT

The Nature and Origin of the New Testament

by

J. MERLE RIFE

PHILOSOPHICAL LIBRARY
New York

Copyright, 1975, by PHILOSOPHICAL LIBRARY, INC.
15 East 40th Street, New York, N. Y. 10016
All rights reserved

Library of Congress Catalog Card No. 74-80276
SBN 8022-2148-3

MANUFACTURED IN THE UNITED STATES OF AMERICA

In Memory of

HAROLD RIDEOUT WILLOUGHBY
*who first introduced me
to these fields*

CONTENTS

I. General Survey 1
   1. The Nature of the New Testament 1
   2. The Septuagint, Bible of the Early Church 3
   3. Jewish Missionary Success 4
   4. Traditions about Jesus 5
   5. The Career of Jesus 9
   6. Development of Ideas About Jesus 9
   7. Authors and Dates 14
   8. The Nuclei of the New Testament 17
   9. The Completion of the New Testament 19
  10. The Apostolic Fathers 20
  11. Copying the Greek Testament by Hand 21
  12. Translation 26
  13. Modern Study of the New Testament 28

II. Paul's Life and Letters 30
   1. Sources, General Summary 30
   2. Missionary Journeys 33
   3. Galatians 37
   4. First Thessalonians 41
   5. Second Thessalonians 43
   6. First Corinthians 44
   7. Second Corinthians 50
   8. Romans 52
   9. Return to Jerusalem 54
  10. Philippians 55
  11. Colossians 56
  12. Philemon 58
  13. The End of Paul's Life 58

CONTENTS (*continued*)

III. THE GOSPEL, ORAL AND WRITTEN 62
    1. The Oral Gospel 62
    2. Mark 69

    3. Matthew 78
    4. Luke-Acts 84
    5. John 92

IV. APOCALYPTIC WRITINGS 101
    1. The Revelation of John 102
    2. The Shepherd of Hermas 108
    3. The Revelation of Peter 113

V. LETTERS AND TREATISES 115
    1. Hebrews 115
    2. Ephesians 117
    3. First Peter 119
    4. First Clement 122
    5. Pastorals (First and Second Timothy, Titus) ... 123
    6. The Letters of Ignatius 127
    7. First, Second, and Third John 132
    8. James 133
    9. Jude 135
    10. Papias 135
    11. Second Peter 136

CONCLUSION 137

APPENDICES 139
    1. Historical Chart 139
    2. Passages Illustrative of Naive Concepts, etc. 141
    3. The Sayings on the Cross 143
    4. Famous Ascension Narratives 144
    5. Outline of Luke's Central Portion 147

INDEX 151

Preface

The following pages are, to a considerable extent, the result of over thirty years of teaching. I have outlined more or less briefly the matters I think should be considered by college students taking a one-semester course, or by any persons interested in the history and ideas of the New Testament.

As in the case of any piece of literature, or other work of art, each individual book should first be allowed to make its own impression. Discussion is secondary. Most of the translation from Greek is my own.

I am under obligation to publishers for permission to quote certain passages which are acknowledged ad loca.

Most of all, gratitude is owed my wife for assistance in proofreading.

J. MERLE RIFE
Amelia, Ohio
June 24, 1974

Test everything, keep what is good.

I Thes. 5:21

CHAPTER I

General Survey

1. THE NATURE OF THE NEW TESTAMENT

The New Testament is a symposium, in twenty-seven articles, on the career and significance of Jesus. In contrast to the writing and assembling of a conventional symposium, this one was composed at various times over a period of a half century or more by men who did not realize their work would some day be part of a collection.

The collecting was a gradual process extending over three centuries as the developing Christian movement came to regard some of its numerous writings as especially useful and inspiring, and as having superior authority. The more important items were agreed on during the first century of the movement, namely, the four Gospels and Paul's letters. By the middle of the second century of the Christian era these were firmly anchored in the life of the Church as part of the ritual of public worship, and are still read to most Christians in the Epistle Lesson and the Gospel Lesson during the liturgy.

The question may be raised whether the Epistle Lesson comes before the Gospel Lesson because Paul's letters are older than the Gospels. But then, how explain the fact that in the New Testament the Gospels come before the Epistles? First, it should be remembered that the program of public worship is older than the New Testament.

Also it must be recognized that the parts of the Bible are not arranged in the order in which they were written. One of the most basic lessons in the history of the Bible is that several

1

conflicting principles operated in determining the arrangement of the various parts, both of the Old Testament and the New. The first consideration was the date of the subject matter. Genesis was put first in the Old Testament because it deals with beginnings, no matter when it was written. Location in the completed volume depended on the subject matter, not on the date of composition. The career of Jesus came before the missionary work of Paul and other disciples, so the Gospels were put before Acts and the letters, no matter when any of them were written.

A second consideration was the length of a writing, a rather strange principle, but it played a large part in the arrangement of both Testaments. In the Old the major prophets come before the minor, being major because longer. In the New Testament Paul's letters are arranged mainly by length,[1] the longer coming before the shorter, regardless of dates. This device is employed by some newspapers, longer editorials coming before shorter.

Yet, in the Bible, the date of writing was not entirely without effect. The Gospel according to John was always considered the last of the four to be written.

A fourth principle determined the position of the so-called Catholic Epistles, namely James, First and Second Peter, First, Second, and Third John, and Jude. These seven little tracts were the last to find a place in the volume, forming an appendix to the epistle section.

The twenty-seven pieces of the New Testament are traditionally known as "books," though a few are only a page or two long. In modern times these "books" were divided into chapters of about a page in length, for convenient daily readings, and the chapters into verses for convenience of reference. That such short compositions should be called books is due partly to the fact that ancient books were written by hand, and that the writing material was thicker than modern paper. But the main reason for the greater bulk was that books were in the form of scrolls, or rolls, rather than leaf books. So what look like chapters in a modern book were bulky scrolls when the New Testament was being written. The Gospel according to Matthew, for in-

---

[1] In two series: letters to churches and letters to individuals arranged according to length.

stance, would require a strip of papyrus about twenty-five feet long, which made a large scroll, but in a modern book Matthew occupies only thirty to sixty pages.

Because of the nature and length of the process by which the writings of the New Testament were selected, it may also be described as the standard collection of early Christian classics, classics being writings that survive over the years and through the centuries.

Another valid characterization of the New Testament is that it is an appendix to the Old Testament. But the Old Testament was written in Hebrew and the New in Greek. How did the Jewish Bible, written in Hebrew, come to have a Greek appendix written for Christians?

The answer, to begin with, is that Greek-speaking Jews, before the Christian era, had translated their Bible into Greek. This translation is perhaps the most important event in the history of western literature, if not of world literature, for it is how we got the Bible, or the first three-fourths of it.

2. The Septuagint, Bible of the Early Church

The history of this momentous translation, known as the Septuagint, may well begin with Alexander the Great, and what happened to Jews after his conquests. The battle of Issus in 333 B.C. is usually taken as the decisive engagement in Alexander's oriental campaign. After this success he advanced down the east coast of the Mediterranean and successfully invaded Egypt. Before leaving for the further east he gave orders for the founding of the city that still bears his name. Beginning as a Greek city it remained an important center of Greek life till the days of Nasser, under whom the Greek population was severely reduced.

Alexandria also became an important center of Jewish life soon after its founding. Immigrants from Palestine to this Greek-speaking city did not maintain the Aramaic speech of their homeland. With the loss of Aramaic went also the knowledge of Hebrew. The two languages are so much alike that knowledge of one makes the other easy. Aramaic-speaking people easily learned to read Hebrew, but Greek is no help; so

3

the Jews of Alexandria and other Greek-speaking cities soon had to have a Greek translation of their Bible.

Their Greek Old Testament is known as the Septuagint, because of the legend that it was made by seventy translators, but no authority attaches to the number seventy. As usual however, the least authentic feature of the tradition was the easiest remembered. In fact, it was done by an unknown number of translators over a period of some two centuries. It was begun in the middle of the third century B.C. with the translation of the Torah, called in Greek the Pentateuch, i.e., "five scrolls." Among modern Christians it is also known as the Mosaic Law. It was translated first because in Judaism it is the most sacred. The Prophets are regarded as next in importance, so were translated next. The rest of the books, known as Writings, or in Greek Hagiographa, were translated before the Christian era, possibly as early as 100 B.C.

For a century the Septuagint was the only Bible Christians had. It is hard for modern Christians to assimilate into their thinking the facts that early Christians spoke mainly Greek, and that their Bible was the Greek Old Testament. The New Testament books were being written, but were not yet regarded as Scripture. Even after they were written it took well over two centuries to get them all corralled into the New Testament. In the meantime the Church simply took over the Bible of the Greek-speaking Synagogue and claimed it as its own.

That the Septuagint was available throughout the Empire was due to Jewish expansion in the whole Mediterranean world, accompanied by successful missionary activity.

3. JEWISH MISSIONARY SUCCESS

By the year 70 there were flourishing Christian congregations in various cities of the Mediterranean world, e.g., Jerusalem, Antioch, Ephesus, Philippi, Thessalonica, Corinth, Rome, etc. The basis for this rapid development was previous Jewish missionary activity. From Acts 15:21 we understand there were Jewish communities in many cities of the Empire. Long before the beginning of Christianity Jews had been active missionaries among gentiles. They traversed sea and land to make one convert, Matthew 23:15. It is part of the all-pervading anti-Semitism of Christian speech to use the word proselyte for converts to Judaism and convert for proselytes to Christianity. In the Greek-speaking areas of the Mediterranean Jews had made many converts. There were also numbers of adherents, people who attended synagogue services, but had not yet joined. Converts were called "devout" and "those who fear God." In Isaiah 56:6-8 they are called "foreigners who attach themselves to the Lord." In Psalms 22:23, 115:9-11, and in Acts 13:16 they are called "those who fear the Lord," and "those who fear God."

Jews had planted the seed throughout the Roman empire and had a crop "ripe for harvesting." The early Christian movement reaped it. The book of Acts presents synagogue preaching as the typical Christian entering wedge. In a new field, we are told, Paul would preach first in the synagogue. The hospitality of synagogues to visiting preachers is also illustrated in Luke 4:14-17, where Jesus preaches in various synagogues as well as in his home town.

At first the difference between Christians and other Jews was in their attitude toward Jesus. Jews had long been looking for the coming of the Messiah (Anointed), in Greek "Christ," who was to usher in a time of peace and righteousness for the whole world. It turned out to be much easier to convince pagans, and Jewish converts from paganism, that Jesus was a promised saviour than to convince native Jews that he was the Messiah, so within a couple of generations the Christian movement was made up mainly of gentiles.

4. TRADITIONS ABOUT JESUS

The chief features of the New Testament are traditions about Jesus, borrowings from the Old Testament, and letters written by Paul the missionary.

Paul's letters are the oldest part of the collection, but have never been considered the most important. The four Gospels come first, both in the table of contents and in the universal regard of Christendom. They are the classic summaries of traditions about Jesus.

It is impossible to say when such traditions were first written down, but we can speculate with some plausibility, first as to why our present Gospels were not composed sooner, and second as to what, with comparative abruptness, precipitated the writing of the first three, Mark, Matthew, and Luke, soon after the year 70.

In regard to the first question it seems clear that the first generation of Christians felt no need of written accounts. They confidently expected Jesus would come again in glory before the eyewitnesses were all gone. Paul, who belonged to the first generation, reminded the Thessalonians in his first letter to them, 1:9, that they had "turned to God from idols, to serve a living and true God, and to await his son from the heavens," and that his (Paul's) purpose was to establish them with blameless and righteous hearts "before our God and father at the coming of our Lord Jesus with all his saints," 3:13, and that "we who are alive at the coming of the Lord will have no advantage over those who have died," 4:15 ff. In First Corinthians 15:51-52 he writes, "We shall not all die, but we shall all be changed, in an instant, in the twinkling of an eye." The Synoptic Gospels record the prediction as follows:

Matthew 16:27-28	Mark 8:38-9:1	Luke 9:26-27
The son of man is going to come in the glory of the father with his angels. And then he will repay each one according to his deeds.	when he comes in the glory of the father with the holy angels.	when he comes in his glory and that of his father and the holy angels.
Really, I tell you, there are some of those standing here who will never taste death until they see the son of man coming in his kingdom.	Really, I tell you, there are some of those standing here who will never taste death until they see the kingdom of God here in power.	And I tell you truly, there are some of those standing here who will never taste death until they see the kingdom of God.

These statements caused some embarrassment later, for the obvious reason that someone had been mistaken, either Jesus or his reporters. Christians have been unwilling to admit either alternative, especially the former. Perhaps that is why Luke

6

17:20-21 reports Jesus saying, "The kingdom of God is not coming visibly." It is no doubt the reason the Gospel of John and other later books pass over the whole subject so lightly. There must have been few, if any, eyewitnesses left by the turn of the century. Oral reports about Jesus and his teaching were by that time all secondhand.

No doubt teachers and preachers had many stereotyped statements which they repeated innumerable times in the manner of present day evangelistic preachers, seldom changing the form of statement, but sometimes adding to it.

In outlining what happened to traditions about Jesus, Professor Benjamin W. Bacon, in *Jesus the Son of God*, made striking use of a scriptural allusion, viz., "What the eye saw, what the ear heard," and "what entered into the heart of man." What the eye saw is the problem of historians, what the ear heard is largely what we have in the Synoptic Gospels, what entered into the heart of man is to be found in the New Testament Letters and the Fourth Gospel. However, the differences among the Synoptics and between them and John are only of degree. Interpretation of the tradition is to be found on every page of each Gospel. As in the case of Paul, it was not only what the writer had heard, but also what he had conceived in meditation and argument.

Anecdotes soon circulate about any prominent character. If the individual is considered important enough the anecdotes are eventually revised and incorporated in biography. Had nothing been written about George Washington until a generation after his death, the surviving oral traditions would, it seems, have been of somewhat the same nature as what the first gospel writer had to work with. A further realization of how oral traditions operate may be gained by thinking of some outstanding character in one's family, some grandparent or uncle who is remembered in family tradition. The stories or anecdotes about such a person circulate as more or less independent units, usually without exact dates, often without even approximate dates. Some are connected with occasions that can be dated.

Our earliest Gospel, that of Mark, is obviously made up of such rather independent and self-contained units.

By the time the earliest gospels were written and the importance of Jesus realized, no one remembered the date of his birth or crucifixion. It was remembered that the Roman governor, Pontius Pilate, had sentenced him to death. Matthew and Luke say he was born while Herod was king. Josephus shows, Antiquities 14.389 and 17.191, that Herod died in the year 4 B.C., so it is generally assumed that Jesus was born at least 4 B.C. However, Luke says, 2:2, that Jesus was born while Quirinius was governor of Syria, while Josephus says, Antiquities 17.342 and 355, that Quirinius came to Syria to take a census after the deposition of Archelaus, i.e., in the year 6 A.D. There seems to be no good reason for preferring Josephus to Luke. It is also possible they were not referring to the same census.

In the sixth century of the Christian era, when the monk Dionysius Exiguus introduced the present system of dating from the birth of Jesus, it was much too late to determine the exact year.

Luke, 3:23, says Jesus was getting to be somewhere in the neighborhood of thirty when he began his ministry. From Josephus, Antiquities 18.2.2. (29-35) and 18.4 (89), it can be calculated that Pilate was procurator of Judea from 26 to 36. Luke 3:1 says John was preaching in the desert in the fifteenth year of Tiberius, which is 29 of the Christian era.

Not much over a generation later, with comparative suddenness, gospels began to be written. At least so it seems. What was the cause of this literary activity? The early Christians were no doubt shocked by the executions of Peter and Paul at Rome in the middle sixties, and also by the destruction of Jerusalem in the year seventy by the Roman army under Titus. These reminders of the passing of the eyewitnesses, and the end of the world they had been looking for, may have precipitated the production of the Synoptics, i.e., Mark, Matthew, and Luke, in all of which the destruction of Jerusalem and the end of the age are so prominent, and so closely connected, and such emphatic statements made that the second coming will take place while some of the eyewitnesses of Jesus' ministry are still living.

8

5. The Career of Jesus

Some forty years before the first destruction of Jerusalem by the Romans, Jesus the Galilean had come to hear John the Baptist preach. It may have been the time of one of the annual festivals, possibly the Passover. He was aroused by John's appeal and accepted his baptism, but did not long remain among his followers.

At some time, perhaps under the influence of John's preaching, Jesus must have had at least one mystic experience. The baptism and transfiguration narratives should be considered in this connexion. It was probably on some such occasion as this that he became convinced that he himself was to have an essential role in the Messianic era. It is widely realized among historians that one of the most difficult problems in the history of Christianity is the self-consciousness of Jesus. Some are convinced that he thought of himself as the Messiah. Christians of course have always taken this for granted.

Jesus started his independent movement in Galilee, with Capernaum as headquarters, engaging in preaching, teaching, and faith healing. His activities were naturally frowned upon by representatives of established religion and by those who felt economically secure. He carried his campaign to Jerusalem, possibly at the next Passover. The Roman authorities were alarmed and arrested him. Pilate held some sort of hearing, apparently consulting Jewish authorities, and ordered his execution.

A few days later some of his intimate friends had visions of Jesus alive, and were convinced of their objectivity. Prominent among those so convinced were Peter and Mary Magdalene.

But why were his former followers now convinced that he was the Anointed? He must have told them so during his brief public career. This was always obvious to Christians, but strongly doubted by some historians.

6. Development of Ideas About Jesus

Almost at once, after Peter and others were convinced that they had seen the living Jesus, a highly emotional movement developed, full of joy, hope, and mutual love, certain that Jesus was the Anointed, certain too that, though invisible except in moments of mystic experience, he was always present among them. It was a contagious enthusiasm, but of only moderate appeal to birthright Jews. It was much more attractive to the numerous gentile converts to Judaism, and to pagans.

Jewish hopes were the basis of Christian ideas about Jesus, hopes for a restoration of national independence, for a supernatural intervention in human affairs that would set things right in this troubled world, an intervention led by a glorious king anointed by God to lead the victorious armies of Israel, and through Israel the whole world, into an age of heavenly perfection. Time and again Jewish hopes were aroused that the time was at hand, just as similar Christian hopes of the second coming of the Anointed have through the centuries often been aroused to fanatical conviction.

It should be clearly understood that *messiah* is the Hebrew word meaning "anointed" and that *christ* is the Greek word. When Jewish scholars translated the Hebrew Bible into Greek they used the Greek word *christ*, but English Bibles do not have it translated into English, so the English reader is left without an important historical clue.

A Jew once wrote me in Yiddish, "What is the difference between Jews and Christians? Jews are looking for the first coming of the Anointed and Christians for the third." (He counted the resurrection as the second.) In the first century some Jews were convinced that Jesus was the Anointed. The majority rejected the idea. A minority of Jews to this day have a vivid hope of the coming of the Messiah, just as a minority of Christians have a lively expectation of his second coming. Standard creedal statements, both Jewish and Christian, continue to affirm belief in the coming of a divinely anointed king who will head a supernatural intervention in world affairs.

It is a belief developed in discouragement and pessimism, a belief conditioned by two convictions: first, that there is a righteous God and that therefore righteousness will eventually triumph; and second, that unaided human efforts are doomed to failure, that left to himself man is going from bad to worse, so the only hope is help from above.

10

In the Old Testament the book of Daniel is the culminating expression of this idea, as the book of Revelation is in the New. Jews and Christians have found many other passages in the Old Testament to support this belief. Some of the passages were never so intended by the authors. Pious people have always been able to find almost anything they want in the Bible, and to find it in almost any place in the sacred text. Christians have interpreted all possible and many impossible passages to mean that Jesus was the Anointed.

In Matthew 1:23 there is a quotation from a Hebrew work of eight centuries earlier, where the ancient Greek translation says, "The virgin will be pregnant and will bear a son and they will name him Immanuel." In the next two verses, clearly referring to the time of Ahaz, in the eighth century B.C., the prophet says that before the boy knows to reject evil and choose the good, the land whose two kings Ahaz feared, would be deserted. All this did not prevent the early Christians from taking the verse as a prophecy of the virgin birth of Christ, especially since the Hebrew word *'almah* had for some unknown reason been translated "virgin" instead of "young woman." Ancient readers like modern were usually looking for agreements, not differences. The most important part of the prophecy is the name Immanuel, three words meaning "God is with us." Isaiah 7:14 has been used regularly through the centuries to support both the doctrine of the virgin birth and the deity of Christ.

In another bit of Hebrew prophecy, Micah 5:2, there is a statement about a pre-existent ruler: "But you, Bethlehem Ephrathah, who are little to be among the thousands of Judah, out of you will come for me one who will be a ruler in Israel, and his outgoings are from ancient times, from everlasting." This is a clear announcement of the pre-existence of the Messiah. Some think it produced the belief that Jesus was born in Bethlehem. Matthew 2:6 quotes it as fulfilled by the birth of Jesus.

Second Isaiah's prophecy, 40:3, of the building of a highway through the desert for the return of the Jews from Babylon is taken in Matthew 3:3 as a prediction of the desert preaching of John.

Early Christian preachers preached Christ, but their Scripture

11

texts had to be found in the Septuagint. This naturally led to some desperate and far-fetched interpretations. We cannot tell whether certain texts suggested beliefs, or the beliefs found in them supporting Scripture.

Zechariah 4:11 describes a vision of two olive trees on opposite sides of a lampstand. This is taken in Revelation 11:4 as a symbol of Moses and Elijah standing beside Jesus at his transfiguration. Some such passages must have been at first merely suggestions that later came to be considered proofs.

The veneration accorded Jesus by his followers was abhorrent to most Jews, although they themselves, at least many living in Greek environments, venerated Abraham, Moses, and other Old Testament worthies, in terms that sound extravagant to Christians. The intrusion of Jesus into a position of similar or greater honor was resented. Moreover, both Jews and Christians in defending their religion were under pressure from pagan competition. Old Testament figures and Jesus were compared to the great figures of Greek and Roman mythology and to deified emperors.

In Graeco-Roman polytheism almost any great man might have divine honors accorded him after death. Livy tells, I.16,20, that Romulus, legendary first king of Rome, was in the first century B.C. worshipped under the name Quirinus. He was popularly believed to be the son of a vestal virgin and the god Mars. It was also believed that he had ascended to heaven without dying, and that he had, after his ascension, appeared to one of his friends to offer encouragement and advice. This was only one of many deified heroes. There were "gods many and lords many."

Such use of the word *god* was far different from the lofty monotheism of Pharisaic Judaism. This strict monotheism was hard to maintain in the Greek world. Many Jews imitated pagan usage by ascribing divine honors to their own ancient heroes. Pagan polytheism made it easier for Christians to deify Jesus. As the Anointed he was by the middle of the first century already regarded by some as the equal of God the father. Paul practically, if not entirely, deifies Jesus, if certain passages in

12

Romans, Second Corinthians, Colossians, and Philemon are his own words and not those of a later editor.

Romans 9:5, as punctuated in older versions, speaks of Christ as God. However the oldest and most reliable manuscripts, Sinaiticus, Vaticanus, and Alexandrinus, as originally written, have no punctuation at all in this verse. So different punctuation, as in some twentieth century translations, is also quite justifiable. In Second Corinthians 4:4 Christ is said to be God's *icon*, i.e., image or picture, a figure that allows some latitude of interpretation. Colossians 1:15-16 presents Christ as the acting agent in the creation of the world. The use of this idea by a later writer, the author of the Fourth Gospel, won for him the title "Holy Theologian," as the clause "through whom all things were made" became standard doctrine. It should be noted that some question the authenticity of the letter to the Colossians. In Philippians 1:2 there is a Binitarian formula, virtually placing God the father and the Lord Jesus Christ on the same level; and in 2:6 f. we read that "Christ Jesus, although existing in the form of God, did not think equality with God something to be clung to, but renounced all and became like a slave."

A word may be said here about the use of names for Jesus. Paul rarely uses the name Jesus alone, oftener in Second Corinthians than in all his other letters together. His most common use is the single title Christ, his most peculiar use is the order Christ Jesus, which is not used anywhere except in the Pauline letters and Acts; but is used most consistently in four writings whose authenticity is suspect, viz., Ephesians, First and Second Timothy, and Titus. In the accepted Paulines Jesus Christ occurs sometimes and sometimes the Lord Jesus. In the Gospels on the contrary, Jesus is used almost exclusively, but Christ also in Luke-Acts and John. We have here one of several straws in the wind that generally confirm modern historical views of date and authorship.

The development of ideas about Jesus may be outlined roughly by saying he was first known as a peasant, then a teacher, sometimes called rabbi, then some came to believe he was the Anointed of prophecy. Since the messiah idea was foreign to pagans, it was soon overshadowed by the God concept as Christianity became more and more exclusively a gentile religion. Christ then became simply a proper name.

However, the influence of Jewish monotheism remained strong, so the idea of one God was forcibly and illogically combined with the idea that Christ had existed from all eternity as God together with the father. A century after Paul, Justin Martyr, the chief source on mid-second century Christianity, could speak in his Apology, 13.3, of Jesus Christ being in the second place, and of the prophetic Spirit "being honored in the third place." The equality of the three persons of the Trinity was not yet standard belief.

7. Authors and Dates

All the New Testament writers, as far as we know, were of Jewish origin, except perhaps Luke, who may have been a gentile convert to Judaism before becoming a Christian. The Bible of all these men was the Septuagint, and they all took for granted its attitude of pious and loving submission to the eternal Spirit, and of unselfish devotion to the welfare of one's fellow men.

They were more or less liberal in their interpretation of Old Testament ritual prescriptions. Paul denied there was any essential obligation to observe any particular form of worship. He considered it a sign of weakness in his less radical brethren that they felt obligated to observe certain ceremonial commandments in the Mosaic Law. At the other extreme we find Matthew reporting a saying of Jesus that not one jot or tittle of the Law will be nullified until it is all fulfilled. The crux here is the word "fulfilled." At any rate, many early Christians, especially in Palestine, felt it was their duty to observe the whole Law. Some modern Protestants have similar attitudes.

The distinctive view of the authors of the New Testament was of course the conviction that Jesus was the fulfillment of Scriptural prophecy, and their main desire was to secure wholehearted allegiance to him as Lord and Savior.

They were all pre-scientific men, untouched by Greek criticism of popular concepts of the world. None of them had a Greek higher education. Luke displays some acquaintance with Greek literature and attitudes, but still considers himself an outsider. Paul makes use of certain Greek philosophical principles, which were no doubt common property generally accepted among Greek-speaking people.

In general it must be stated that New Testament writers believed in ghosts, supposed the sky was a solid dome only a few hundred feet above the earth, and the floor of heaven immediately above this ceiling; and assumed that angels could come down quite conveniently from the upper story and move either seen or unseen among men; that beneath the earth was hell, peopled with evil spirits that came up just as easily and naturally as angels came down; and that diseases both physical and mental were caused by these evil spirits. One writer believed that an infant could sin even before it was born, and another that an unborn child could be inspired by the Holy Spirit. Gross anthropomorphism prevailed in popular concepts of deity, though exalted spiritual views appear here and there. Passages illustrating the statements of this paragraph are given in Appendix II.

Religions are usually, if not always, founded by mystics. An ecstatic seizure, a mount of transfiguration, is the focal point from which spreads a phenomenal burst of energy, sweeping like fire into the life of susceptible persons and communities. Such ecstasies are not usually for the intelligentsia or the sophisticated. "Not many of high standing in learned or government circles," as Paul terms them, are attracted by such movements. But they spread among the humble and unpretentious. Some at least of the New Testament writers were mystics, and they believed in the objective reality of things seen in visions.

There is no doubt of the fact of visions. Even the most skeptical sometimes have visions so vivid that they can hardly convince themselves they have not seen actual objective appearances. The basic fallacy of the credulous is the conviction that mystic experience validates views and theories held or arrived at during ecstasy. Consider Moses, Buddha, Paul, Augustine of Hippo, Muhammad, Joan of Arc, Martin Luther, and others.

15

Mystic experiences are real, but they are not proof of the reality of things seen during the seizure.

Much misunderstanding has arisen from the practice of some authors of using an assumed name. There are various motives for this literary device, ranging from diffidence to dishonesty. A British author in the first half of this century wrote a quasi-autobiography of a Roman emperor, entitled *I Claudius*. There was no intention to deceive. We may assume equal innocence on the part of an unknown Jewish author who shortly before the Christian era wrote the book of *Enoch* in the first person. Another unknown Jewish author about 165 B.C. wrote a book in the name of Daniel, a traditional hero who had lived a few centuries earlier. It is doubtful whether any contemporary readers were misled. Coming down into Christian times we may say the same of a tract written in the second century and bearing the name Peter. Only the more ignorant of contemporary readers could have misunderstood; but a generation or two later some prominent Christians regarded it as the work of the apostle. A large part of the Church still thought it pseudonymous. It was more than two centuries before it won general acceptance as an apostolic writing. Modern historians have shown there are several other books in the New Testament that were not written by the men popularly believed to be the authors. These beliefs developed partly through lack of historical judgment, partly through wishful thinking. The books were good, therefore they must have been written by apostles. Moreover the unfortunate and arbitrary criterion had been adopted that no book without apostolic authority could be included in the Bible; so it was a question of losing some good books or turning a deaf ear to history. Popular Christianity has usually preferred the latter course.

The oldest New Testament document is one of Paul's letters, either Galatians or First Thessalonians, the latter being the only New Testament book whose date is definitely known, i.e., about the year 50. The indications are that Paul suffered martyrdom at Rome in the middle sixties.

Mark, our earliest Gospel, seems to have been written soon after the destruction of Jerusalem, which was in the year 70.

16

Within the next twenty years Matthew, a revised edition of Mark, came out, and the more ambitious work, Luke-Acts was produced, making extensive use of Mark in the first volume, and in the second incorporating parts of a travel document composed by one of Paul's companions, perhaps by Luke himself.

Revelation and the treatise known as Hebrews seem to have been written before the end of the first century, the remaining books before the middle of the second. Last of all, it seems, was Second Peter.

Each of the New Testament books is discussed in some detail in later chapters.

8. THE NUCLEI OF THE NEW TESTAMENT

Two separate nuclei were assembled before there was a New Testament as such. The first nucleus was a collection of Paul's letters, and its formation was closely connected with the development of a fixed form of worship.

It has always been permissible to read current letters at regular services, Jewish or Christian; and we know that Paul expected some of his letters to be read in church, e.g., First Thessalonians 5:27, "I adjure you by the Lord to have this letter read to all the brothers." Sometimes he requested that a given letter be read to more than one congregation, e.g., Colossians 4:16, "Salute the brothers and Nympha, and the church at her house. And when the letter has been read before you, cause it also to be read in the church at Laodicea and you read the one from Laodicea." As far as we know this was the first time any of his letters was read in more than one church. Possibly each of these churches copied its letter before sending it on, and so had the beginning of a Pauline letter collection.

Christian worship was at first an informal adaptation of synagogue worship, which included the reading of formal Scripture lessons. We do not know how formal the Old Testament lessons were in the early Church, or how soon the reading of epistles was systematized; but we know that by the middle of the second century both Old Testament lessons and the writings of

Christian missionaries were being read regularly. We learn this from chapter 67 of Justin Martyr's Apology. Due to the expensiveness of hand-copied books, it is likely that most laymen acquired their knowledge of Scripture from church readings. Usage in worship probably played the major part in the growth of the New Testament. Mission documents gradually became sacred because they were heard in church.

Sooner or later a collection of Paul's letters was put into circulation. John Knox has argued persuasively that it was Onesimus,[1] bishop of Ephesus, who did this, and that he was the same Onesimus about whom Paul wrote to Philemon, 1.10. A generation later Polycarp, to whom Ignatius had written, had a collection of the letters of Ignatius to send to the Philippians.

A second New Testament nucleus grew from the Gospel of Mark, of which Matthew is a revised edition. Mark was also extensively used in the composition of Luke. To these three Gospels was finally added the Fourth, "according to John." Mark seems to have been preserved more as a relic than anything else, for there was little incentive to read it when Matthew was available. Only in modern times, and among historical students, has Mark become popular.

A third and less coherent nucleus consists of apocalypses, viz., the Revelation of John, the Shepherd of Hermas, and the Revelation of Peter. For a time each of these had its advocates, but only one managed to survive as part of the Bible, the Revelation of John, and through the centuries many have objected to it.

The fourth and latest nucleus is the Catholic Epistles, viz., James, First and Second Peter, First, Second, and Third John, and Jude. These seven pamphlets, together with Revelation, were the last of the twenty-seven books to be accepted as Scripture. In the fourth century there were still leading Christians who thought some of the Catholic Epistles did not belong in the Bible, and for at least a century longer there were those who included certain other books beside the twenty-seven.

---

[1] *Philemon among the Letters of Paul.* Chicago. 1935.

9. THE COMPLETION OF THE NEW TESTAMENT

Marcion usually gets the credit for first recognizing certain New Testament books as Scripture, and for assembling the first rudimentary New Testament. This was in the middle of the second century. Marcion was an anti-Semite, and proposed to discard the Jewish Bible in favor of one containing only Christian writings, the very thing many modern Christians do by reading or owning only the New Testament.

The ancient Church did not accept Marcion's radical proposal. In the course of the next two centuries it accepted even more Christian writings than Marcion had, but did not discard the Septuagint. Marcion in disappointment left the Catholic Church and founded what may be called the first Protestant Church. For use in his church he compiled a bible containing the Gospel according to Luke and ten Pauline letters, though he removed certain passages from the Gospel. The present list of twenty-seven books appeared for the first time, as far as we know, in the year 367, when Athanasius, Patriarch of Alexandria, Egypt, wrote a pastoral letter to the churches under his jurisdiction authorizing the present list. Even then his decision was not universally accepted.

The main decisions however had been made two centuries earlier. The struggle with heresies resulted in enhancement of the authority of the original missionaries, usually known by the Greek term *apostles*. Before a book was officially accepted by the Church it had to show some connection with an apostle, i.e., one of Jesus' personal appointees. The requirement was sometimes met by a claim of apostolic authorship, as in the case of Matthew and John. Matthew was declared apostolic by Sextus I, bishop of Rome early in the second century, soon after the martyrdom of Ignatius. John was recognized at Rome as apostolic in the latter half of the second century, soon after Polycarp's visit there. Secondhand apostolic authority was sufficient for Mark and Luke, each of these men having been a companion of Paul. Luke is so identified in both Colossians and Philemon; Acts reports Mark's association with Paul. However, Paul's claim to apostleship was attacked. His most vehement defense

19

is in Galatians. Toward the middle of the second century Papias wrote that Mark had been Peter's interpreter at Rome. Not all such claims were convincing. The Revelation of Peter and Acts of Paul were rejected. However, if a book seemed especially valuable, the claims of apostolic authority were more easily believed, as in the case of the Fourth Gospel.

Origen was the greatest Christian scholar of the early centuries. Writing in the first half of the third he accepted First Peter, but rejected Second Peter. He also rejected the Gospel, Acts, Preaching, and Revelation of Peter. He accepted fourteen letters of Paul, but recognized the doubtful authorship of Hebrews. He was inclined to reject the Shepherd of Hermas, though recognizing it as a useful book.

In the fourth century Eusebius, known as the father of church history, gives summaries of attitudes on New Testament books in his day, some universally accepted, some everywhere rejected, and some still argued about, Church History 3.2-4. The Catholic Epistles had all been suspected.

Further evidence on the developing contents of the New Testament is found in the two oldest extant complete Bibles, both now in the British Museum in London. The older, Codex Sinaiticus, was produced in the fourth century, soon after Christianity had been legalized in the Empire and made one of the official religions. The other, Codex Alexandrinus, was produced in the fifth century. These Bibles were of course written by hand, over a thousand years before the beginning of printing in the western world. They are written on parchment, i.e., skin of sheep or antelopes. The writing is in capital letters with no spaces between the words. The language is Greek, the Old Testament being the Septuagint version. Each of these ancient Bibles has twenty-nine books in its New Testament, the two extra in Sinaiticus being the Epistle of Barnabas and the Shepherd of Hermas; in Alexandrinus the two extra are First and Second Clement, all four among the Apostolic Fathers.

10. The Apostolic Fathers

The small collection of early Christian writers that stands nearest the New Testament is known as the Apostolic Fathers.

The name was based on the assumption that these men lived early enough to be acquainted with some of the original apostles. This was a mistake. Nevertheless, only the New Testament contains more important sources for the history of early Christianity. Most of the Apostolic Fathers wrote before the middle of the second century. They sometimes mention New Testament writers and books, sometimes they quote, but rarely exactly. More often they loosely refer to passages. Some of the Apostolic Fathers, as stated above, have themselves been considered part of the New Testament, e.g., First Clement, a letter written in the middle nineties to the church at Corinth by Clement, bishop of Rome. He says in the letter that he is following Paul's example in writing to them.

Further discussion of the Apostolic Fathers is reserved for Chapters IV and V.

11. Copying The Greek Testament by Hand

All copies of the Greek New Testament made before 1514 were written by hand. In that year Cardinal Ximenez of Spain started the printing of a three-column Bible. In the Old Testament the three columns were respectively Hebrew, Latin, and Greek. In the New Testament the first column was Syriac. In 1516 John Froben, a Basel publisher, printed a volume containing only the Greek New Testament. He had secured the Renaissance scholar Erasmus to prepare the text.

Printing at once revolutionized the process of transmitting the text. During the centuries of hand copying it had departed further and further from the originals. This is because hardly anyone can copy a whole page, let alone a book, without making a mistake. Before printing no two copies of any book were exactly alike, but with printing an unlimited number of copies can be produced with exactly the same wording and spelling.

After printing provided a uniform text, scholars began the long process of detecting the numerous errors of fourteen centuries of hand copying. The process of restoring original wording and spelling is called *textual criticism*. Nearly 5,000 handwritten copies of parts or all of the Greek New Testament have been preserved and brought to the attention of scholarship. Specialists have compared many of them letter by letter with standard printed editions, and recorded every variation. As might be expected, they have found some manuscripts more accurate than others, the oldest usually being the least corrupt. Finally, in the past century they have begun to publish Greek Testaments with the more nearly original readings. The chief bases for these new and more correct editions are the two oldest known Bibles, Sinaiticus and Vaticanus. A brief description of some of the oldest and most valuable manuscripts follows.

Papyri 45, 46, *and* 47 are parts of three third-century papyrus manuscripts from Egypt that have come to the attention of scholars within the past century. The oldest, P,[46] from early in the century, consists of 86 leaves of Pauline letters, 30 leaves at the University of Michigan and 56 leaves in the A. Chester Beatty Library in Dublin. P,[45] from the middle of the century, includes 30 leaves from Matthew, Mark, Luke and John and is located in the Beatty Library. P[47] is 10 leaves of Revelation from the latter part of the century, these also in the Beatty Library.

The texts of these papyri resemble first one and then another of the following great uncials. Uncial means written in capital letters.

Codex Sinaiticus, so called because it is a leaf book and was discovered on the Sinaitic pennsula, was originally a complete Bible. The New Testament is still complete, including the Epistle of Barnabas and part of the Shepherd of Hermas. The material is parchment.

The discoverer was Professor Constantine Tischendorf of the University of Leipzig. He discovered part of the manuscript in 1844 and the rest fifteen years later. It had been in the Greek Orthodox monastery of St. Catherine, but he deposited it in the Royal Library at St. Petersburg, his searches having been financed by the Tsar. In 1933 the British nation and government bought it from the Soviet government for a hundred thousand pounds. Since then it has been in the British Museum in London. It was produced in the fourth century.

Codex Vaticanus is so named because it first came to the

notice of scholars in the Vatican Library at Rome, where it is still located. It is listed in the earliest catalog of the Vatican Library, 1475. It was originally a complete Greek Bible, but the New Testament from Hebrews 9:14 on is now missing. It too is a fourth century uncial written on parchment.

Codex Alexandrinus is another complete Greek Bible, including First and Second Clement in its New Testament. This parchment uncial manuscript is supposed to have been brought to Constantinople by Cyril Lucar in 1621 when he became Ecumenical Patriarch. In 1627 he presented it to Charles I of England. It became part of the Royal Library, which in 1757 was incorporated in the British Museum. It was produced in the fifth century.

Codex Washingtoniensis, so named because now in Washington, D. C., is a fifth century parchment uncial of the Four Gospels. It was bought from an Arab dealer at Gizeh, near Cairo, Egypt, in 1906 by Charles Freer, and is now in the Freer Gallery of the Smithsonian Institution.

Ephraemi rescriptus is called rescriptus because its uncial biblical text was partly erased, and a work of Ephraem the Syrian written over it in cursive, i.e., running hand. After belonging to various Italian and French nobility and royalty it finally reached the French Royal Library, which was later incorporated in the Bibliothèque Nationale in Paris. It is a fifth century parchment manuscript containing parts of each Testament.

Codex Bezae was once the property of the Swiss reformer Théodore de Bèze, who in 1581 presented it to the Cambridge University Library. It is a bilingual parchment uncial of the Gospels, with Greek on the left at each opening and Latin on the right. It was produced in the fifth or sixth century.

Although the above uncials contain a superior text, it is recognized that the Old Latin and Old Syriac translations are from still older forms of the Greek text. We also have writings of the Church Fathers who lived before the fourth century. Their Scripture quotations are often from an older Greek text than that of any known manuscript, while others use the Old Syriac and Old Latin versions representing an older text.

It is not to be expected that the original text will ever be completely restored, but the results of textual criticism may be said to be an improving variable approaching perfection as a limit.

The practical result of all this painstaking labor and endless concern for purity of text is that a modern translator has a more accurate base to work from. When the King James translators did their work, more than three centuries and a half ago, they had the Textus Receptus, a Greek text produced in the previous century, and containing the accumulated errors of over fourteen centuries of hand copying. Today translators have a Greek Testament based on the great uncials, with only three centuries of hand copying back of them. Present day printed Greek Testaments, e.g., of Westcott and Hort and of Nestle-Aland, benefit from four centuries of textual criticism.

Those unable to read Greek can get a fair idea of the differences between the Renaissance and modern Greek texts by comparing the King James version with almost any twentieth century translation, such as the American Revised, Twentieth Century, Moffatt, Weymouth, Goodspeed, Revised Standard, etc., though even these sometimes seem reluctant to follow the findings of textual scholarship.

In this connexion it seems advisable to give a few examples of the more striking variants in each of the Gospels. In Mark they are found in the last chapter. Different manuscripts of this Gospel have four different endings. There is substantial agreement up to the ninth verse of the last chapter. Beginning here there is striking disagreement. The best form of the text ends with the eighth verse: "for they were afraid." The other three endings are different ancient attempts to piece out the apparently incomplete story. The three false endings are of quite different lengths. The King James translators knew only the middle-sized ending, and were unaware of its apocryphal nature. Some modern translations give both the middle-sized and short endings. Codex Washingtoniensis has the long one. Sinaiticus and Vaticanus end with the eighth verse. Ephraemi and Bezae have the middle-sized appendix, which was known to Irenaeus, a late second century Greek father. Codex regius, at the Bibliotheque Nationale, has both the short and middle-sized endings.

The most prominent variant in Matthew is the doxology appended to the Our Father, or Lord's Prayer, viz., "For yours is the kingdom and the power and the glory forever." This doxology is not used in the Roman Catholic Church, nor is it in the Latin Bible, but is the priest's response in the liturgy of the Eastern Orthodox Church. It is likely that some Greek copyist regarded it as part of the prayer, along with the Amen sung by the choir, as he had always heard it in church. The Latin translation was made before these two bits of Greek liturgy got into the Gospel. Washingtoniensis is the earliest known manuscript containing it. It is omitted by Sinaiticus, Vaticanus, Bezae, Dublensis, and many others.

The most striking variants in Luke are in parts of the passion narrative, particularly 22:43-44, where Jesus in the Garden of Gethsemane "sweat as it were great drops of blood," and an angel appears to him; also the saying on the cross, 23:34, "Father forgive them, because they don't know what they are doing." The bloody sweat and the angel are missing in Alexandrinus, Vaticanus, Mosquensis, and the Sahidic fragment; Sinaiticus marks the passage as controversial. "Father forgive them" is absent from Vaticanus and questioned in Sinaiticus and Bezae. It is also absent in certain other manuscripts.

The most striking variant in John is the passage about the woman caught in adultery, at the beginning of the eighth chapter. It is absent from all Greek manuscripts of the Gospel before the eighth century, except Bezae. It is not in the Lord's Day Gospel Lesson from this part of John as read in the Greek Church, but is used for the Gospel Lesson on St. Pelagia's Day. We learn from Eusebius, Church History 3:39.17, that it was taken from the apocryphal Gospel of the Hebrews.

Most textual variants are far less striking than the famous examples given above. Many are mere variations from standard orthography, some are reversals of words, e.g., Matthew 10:2, where one Greek manuscript has "the one called Simon Peter," instead of "Simon, the one called Peter." Some consist of the omission or inclusion of a single word, and most variants have no practical effect on their respective passages. Nevertheless, scholarship seeks the nearest possible approach to perfection. It has been scholars, rather than clergy, who have guarded the words of the Bible, though of course many of the clergy have been scholars too.

12. TRANSLATION

There is little doubt that the mother tongue of Jesus and his disciples was Aramaic, a language closely related to Hebrew, and in fact called Hebrew in the New Testament. There is equally little doubt that Jesus and his more intimate friends heard some Greek, and that they acquired a modicum of this language, though it is hardly likely they learned to read it. We may be fairly sure that the earliest oral traditions about Jesus were in Aramaic. Bilingual preachers such as Paul, Barnabas, and Mark, readily repeated in Greek what they had heard in Aramaic. By the middle of the first century the oral traditions about Jesus were no doubt more widely spread in Greek than in Aramaic.

A few scholars have argued that the Gospels were originally written in Aramaic, but most of their colleagues have disagreed. No one questions the assumption that Paul wrote in Greek, though he too spoke Aramaic, whether learned from his parents in the Greek-speaking city of Tarsus, or from his teachers and companions in Jerusalem. Whether any of the traditions about Jesus were first written down in Aramaic, we do not know, except for the few fragments in the New Testament, viz., *talitha qum,* Mark 5:41; *effetha,* Mark 7:34; *maran atha,* I Corinthians 16:22; and *abba,* Mark 14:36, Romans 8:15, Galatians 4:6; and the statement of Papias that Matthew wrote down the sayings of Jesus in Hebrew. It is certain that the first New Testament, as a collection, was entirely Greek, despite the claim of certain people to have the original Gospels in the language Jesus spoke.

The earliest translations of the New Testament seem to have been from Greek into Syriac and Latin. Syriac is a form of Aramaic, and is still spoken by some Near Eastern Christians. Translations were made into both Syriac and Latin by the end of the second century.

To most of us it seems strange that the first Latin translations of the Bible were made for the use of Roman colonies in North Africa. The Church at Rome used Greek till the third century. Christian Latin first developed in North Africa. The earliest extant Christian author in this language was Tertullian, born in Carthage about 169. He has been called "the founder of ecclesiastical Latinity." The prominent Latin Father and martyr bishop, Cyprian, was an African, as was the greatest of the Latin fathers, Augustine of Hippo. By the fourth century the Church at Rome had become Latin-speaking, and its scholars felt the need of a revised Latin Bible. The revision was the work of Jerome, who learned Hebrew, studied Aramaic, and did much of the work in Palestine. His version was completed in 405. Like some other revisions of the Bible, it met a great deal of opposition, but finally, except for the Psalter, became the standard Bible and official version of the Roman Church. It is known as the *Vulgate*.

Earlier forms of the Bible in Latin are known as the *Old Latin*. The Old Latin Old Testament was translated from the Septuagint, but the Vulgate is more or less conformed to the Hebrew. Jerome's Psalter based on the Hebrew was rejected; only in the middle of the twentieth century has the Catholic Church adopted a Latin version of the Psalms from the Hebrew.

After the Septuagint, the Vulgate is the most important of Bible translations. It was western Christendom's only Bible for a thousand years. One of the first books printed in Europe is the edition of the Vulgate known as the Gutenberg Bible. The Vulgate is still one of the official Bibles of half the world's Christians. The earliest translations into French, German, and English were made from it. Later English revisers, though working with the original languages, i.e., Hebrew and Greek, have never entirely escaped the Vulgate influence.

The King James, or Ancient Version, published in 1611, probably has been read by more people than any other form of the Bible. Although other greatly improved translations are now available, the majority of English-speaking readers still cling to its antiquated, often awkward, phraseology as tenaciously as they clung to their equally awkward and antiquated inches, feet, and yards.

13. MODERN STUDY OF THE NEW TESTAMENT

Hardly any field of history has been worked by so many competent scholars as has that of the New Testament. The competence of many has been more or less hampered by prejudice. Many have labored devotedly and determinedly to prove traditional views correct. Others have been accused of equal bias in trying to prove them wrong. Many who began their studies while holding traditional views have been forced to give up certain positions because of what seemed convincing evidence.

The most crucial question in the history of the New Testament is the authorship of the Fourth Gospel. Most Christians have taken for granted that it was written by John, the son of Zebedee. This Gospel, more than any other writing, has been the basis of their beliefs about the person and nature of Christ. It makes a great deal of difference whether the words ascribed to Jesus are being reported by an eyewitness and intimate friend, or are the formulations of a third generation Christian who never saw Jesus.

In spite of all such historical questions, the epic quality of the New Testament must be recognized. Moreover it is the most widely read book, the one translated into the most languages, and the one most influential in western civilization, a decisive factor in multitudes of lives all over the world.

How can we explain these facts? They constitute one of the major phenomena of human history, involving one-third of the world's population. Perhaps the key word is emotion, emotion combining admiration, love, and gratitude, in response to demonstrations of unselfish personal concern. The object of the emotion is of course the Jesus of the Gospels, viewed with childlike, uncritical trust, the Jesus who says, "Come to me all you who are weary and heavily burdened, and I will give you rest."

The original disciples had learned to admire, love, and trust a man of impressive personality, of complete unselfishness, full of compassion for all in trouble and need, taking a genuine personal interest in individuals. Who is there who is not emotionally affected, at least in certain moods, to find there is someone who cares, someone who cares for me? One must form such emotional attachment when a child, or as a child, in simple unquestioning response to warm, friendly attention. "Unless you become like little children, you cannot enter the kingdom of heaven," says the Christ of the Synoptic Gospels. "Let little children come to me, and don't hinder them, for of such is the kingdom of heaven." It is like the attachment a child has for a revered parent or teacher, or once a year for the benevolent superman, Santa Claus.

The Gospels contain a variety of appeals, those a child can grasp and those suitable for the more mature. A summary of the Gospel presentation for the more thoughtful is found in the Fourth Gospel, 3:16, "For God loved the world so much that he gave his only son, so that whoever believes in him will not perish, but have eternal life." Here God is no longer thought of as a superman, but as the eternal spirit and first cause of all existence, invisible, with no bodily form or material attributes, who in some mysterious way sent a personal manifestation of his nature to live among men as a man, and by his sacrificial death to make eternal life possible for all who will accept.

I once saw from across a room a painting of a pretty little landscape beside a body of water, but when I came close to the picture all the beauty vanished. Nothing was left but some coarse strokes of paint daubed on apparently at random. When I backed away a short distance the picture reappeared.

So it is with the Gospels. The historian with his paste and scissors, with the tools of his historical method, attempting to sort out the scraps, is in no position to feel the overwhelming emotional appeal of the Christ that is felt by so many readers. It is with more or less disgust that the fervent believer observes the activities of the scholar. A man who had been through the Welsh revival and had felt its power, and who had just visited a class studying the Synoptic problem, after describing the revival to me, exclaimed, "Can you do that with documents?" There is a vast difference between belief in a living person and dissecting his corpse.

CHAPTER II

Paul's Life and Letters

1. Sources, General Summary

The oldest "books" in the New Testament are certain letters written by Paul. These are the primary sources for his life. We begin an examination of them by begging one of the main questions of New Testament study, namely, which letters did he write? Pending further examination we assume he wrote Romans, First and Second Corinthians, Galatians, Philippians, Colossians, First and Second Thessalonians, and Philemon. Some authorities think this list too long, while others consider it too short.

The next most important source for Paul's life is the book of Acts, We Sections, 16:10-18, 20:5-16, 21:1-25, and 27:1-28:16, ranking above the rest on the assumption they are the reports of an eyewitness.

Then one must glean the Pastoral and Catholic Epistles and the Apostolic Fathers for what they have to offer.

Finally the general history of the Roman Empire in the first century is indispensable background, its government, social life, geography, chronology, and archeology explaining and clarifying the main sources at every turn.

The Apostle always refers to himself by his Latin name Paul, while in Acts the Hebrew name Saul is used fifteen times in the section 7:58-13:9. In 13:9 Paul is said to be his other name. This is the first occurrence of the name Paul, which is used exclusively in the rest of Acts, 125 times in all. This seems one feature of the author's plan to show how the Church, though starting among Jews, soon became a gentile organization.

30

Although Paul never mentions Tarsus in his own writings, it is given in Acts 9:11, 21:39, and 22:3 as his place of origin. Note that none of these references are in the we sections. Yet Paul makes it clear in Galatians 1:21-2:1 that he was a missionary in the Tarsus region longer than anywhere else.

Paul lays more stress on his Jewish origin than Acts does, e.g., Second Corinthians 11:22, "Are they Hebrews? So am I, etc.;" Romans 11:1, "For I too am an Israelite, one of the descendants of Abraham, and from the tribe of Benjamin;" Philippians 3:4-5, "If anyone has confidence in his pedigree, I can more than match it, circumcised the eighth day, belonging to the race of Israel and the tribe of Benjamin, a Hebrew of the Hebrews;" Galatians 1:13-14, "You have heard of my former practice of Judaism . . . how extremely zealous I was in the observance of the ancestral traditions." In Acts 22:3 we are told that he received a rabbinical education in Jerusalem.

According to Acts 9:1-6 and 22:6-7, it was while on a mission of persecution that he experienced his revolutionary conversion. Both Galatians 1:17 and the above passages in Acts give the vicinity of Damascus as the location of this event. He apparently refers to it in Galatians 1:12-16, "For I did not receive it (his gospel) from man, neither was I taught it, but it was through a revelation of Jesus Christ."

Some ten years later he had a vision reported in Second Corinthians 12:2-4, "I know a man in Christ Jesus who fourteen years ago—whether in the body or out of the body, I do not know, God knows—such a man was snatched up to the third heaven. And I know such a one, whether in the body or outside the body, God knows, that he was snatched into Paradise and heard unutterable words which are impossible for a human being to express."

Necessity of defending his apostleship seems to have been the reason for his emphasis on the original vision. His opponents must have argued that he had never seen Jesus, much less been appointed a missionary by him. The Damascus experience was for him the commission to the apostolate. Had his authority never been attacked he might not have mentioned it in his letters. Furthermore, his emphasis on it must have affected his

Christology, as a similar defense has affected the thinking and beliefs of other Christians before and since.

There is considerable uncertainty in the chronology of Paul's life. We do not know the date of his birth, conversion, or death. He must have been born about the beginning of the century. In Acts 7:58 it is stated that he was a young man at the time of Stephen's martyrdom. Clement of Rome, 5.5-7, seems to support the tradition that Paul himself suffered martyrdom under Nero. In Philemon 9 Paul calls himself an old man. We may assume his conversion took place between 27 and 30. Pilate was procurator of Judea from 26 to 36. We may take 27 as the earliest possible date for his conversion.

His mission as he understood it was to convince both Jews and heathen that a new era had been inaugurated by the death and resurrection of Jesus Christ, and that the only hope for true happiness in this life and in the life to come was to find salvation in union with Christ. He therefore tried to convince Jews that Jesus was the Christ, and that his atoning death on the cross had freed them from all obligation to observe the ritual commandments of the Bible. Gentiles who had not been influenced by Judaism were approachable through their own religious and ethical convictions. They were urged to "turn from idols and serve the living and true God," and to know the joy of being united with his son.

Paul had a clear realization of the distinction between ritual and ethics, and was insistent that his converts from heathenism obey the moral teachings of the Jewish Scriptures. He emphasized that their basic principle is best stated in Leviticus 19:18, "You must love your neighbor as yourself." So thoroughly was early Christianity indoctrinated with this commandment that most Christians today believe the words originated with Jesus.

Paul clearly stated in the fourteenth chapter of Romans, as well as in First Corinthians and Galatians, his principle that no ritual act has any validity in and of itself. At the same time he would avoid offending any "weaker brother" who has scruples about such things. In practice he endorsed the observance of baptism, under the Christian interpretation of the rite, and the solemn sharing of bread and wine as a commemoration of the death of the Lord Jesus. He also gave instructions for the conduct of Christian group worship. Evidence on which the preceding summary is based will be presented later in this chapter.

2. The "Journeys"

Approximately half of Paul's missionary career was fourteen years spent in the "regions" of Syria and Cilicia. We know no details of his work during this period. None of his extant letters are to communities visited during these years, unless the "regions" could be stretched to include the home of the Galatians.

The second phase of his missionary career was the great western project in which he seems to have planned the evangelization of the northern coast of the Mediterranean. We have no statement of his plans further than Spain. His work in the gentile world would be limited to communities where the Greek language was spoken.

On the basis of the account in Acts the mission to the west has usually been divided into three "journeys," and a final imprisonment, the last including travel by sea to Italy.

The first journey consisted of a tour through Cyprus and south central Asia Minor: Perga, Pisidian Antioch, Iconium, Lystra, and Derbe. A rather uniform pattern is presented in Acts: of Paul speaking in synagogues, dividing Jewish congregations, and leaving town amid scenes of violence.

The plan of the second journey was to visit the communities where Paul had been before. At first Silas, Barnabas, and John, alias Mark, were with him; but Paul and Barnabas quarreled over the presence of Mark, so Barnabas and Mark left the others and went back to Cyprus.

Paul and Silas went to Derbe and Lystra, where they met Timothy, son of a Jewish mother and gentile father. Paul wanted to take him along, so had him circumcised out of consideration for the Jews in the region. This account seems in flat contradiction to Galatians 2:3 ff., but Paul's own letters are sometimes inconsistent with each other, especially when he abandons a general principle for the sake of a present expedi-

33

ency; so we need not rule out the testimony of Acts on this ground alone.

They next passed through the Phrygian and Galatian country, but were "prevented by the Spirit" from preaching the gospel in Asia, so went to Troas.

It is in connexion with Troas that the first we section begins, so it seems Luke joined Paul there and accompanied him to Philippi in response to a "vision of the night" in which a man from Macedonia was calling for help. Next they went to Thessalonica, no doubt by the Egnatian Road, either walking or riding donkeys. This important Roman highway finally stretched from Dyrrachium on the Adriatic to Constantinople. Sections of it are still preserved.

As from Philippi, so from Thessalonica, there was the usual violent exit; but at Berea, the next stop, the Jews were more receptive. From Berea Paul started for Corinth, but sent Timothy to Thessalonica while he waited at Athens, First Thessalonians 3:1. Although the visit in Athens was only incidental, Paul did some synagogue and agora preaching. The best known feature of his stay at Athens is his address at the Areopagus, which was probably not the traditional spot shown tourists, with its bronze plate bearing the Greek of Acts 17:22-31.

It seems Paul finally went on to Corinth before Timothy arrived. This would mean that First Thessalonians was written from Corinth. It was probably early in the year 50, as will be explained further on.

As usual Paul's first preaching in Corinth was in a synagogue. It was not long before the controversy resulting from his campaign forced him and his partisans to move to another meeting place. They had the effrontery to meet in a house next door to the synagogue, the home of one of their number, a convert to Judaism named Titius Justus. Crispus, president of the synagogue, also followed Paul. The campaign continued for over a year and a half.

Upon the arrival of Gallio, the new Roman proconsul, probably about the middle of the year 51, the synagogue haled Paul into court, charging him with teaching contrary to the Law. Gallio dismissed the charges as of no interest to the Roman administration. The crowd then seized Sosthenes, the new president of the synagogue, and beat him right in the courtroom. One wonders whether the writer intended to imply this violence was committed by the Christians. This seems the more probable inference.

Not long after this disturbance Paul left Corinth accompanied by Priscilla and Aquila, who had recently come from Rome due to the expulsion of Jews from the city by the emperor Claudius, Acts 18:1-2. Suetonius says, in Claudius 25, that the expulsion was because the Jews continually made disturbances "on the instigation of Chrestus."

Leaving Corinth Paul and his companions sailed from Cenchreae, where Paul had a haircut on account of a vow. They stopped at Ephesus, where Priscilla and Aquila stayed. Paul promised to return, and went on to Antioch by way of Caesarea and Jerusalem. This was the end of the second journey.

The third journey started at Antioch, passed through Galatia and Phrygia, and consisted mainly of a prolonged mission at Ephesus.

When he arrived at Ephesus Paul found a small group of followers of John the Baptist, and made Christians of them. Acts also states that Aquila and Priscilla, in the synagogue at Ephesus, heard a man named Apollos, whose preaching they admired, but whose doctrine they disagreed with. They took him home and set him straight. Then Apollos went to Corinth. The most significant statement about him is that he knew no baptism but John's. There are other traces of a strong following of John the Baptist, showing that for a time it rivalled the following of Jesus. Whether it was completely absorbed by the Christian movement is not certain.

Distinct evidence of the rivalry is seen in the gospel scenes relating to the two leaders, and in the special effort the Fourth Gospel makes, 1:10-34, to convince the reader that Jesus is greater than John. Evidences of the power of the Baptist movement persist to this day. In the standard iconography of the Greek Orthodox Church it is John the Baptist who has the place of honor next after Jesus and Mary among the pictures on the altar screen. Jesus and John stand side by side south of the

Beautiful Gate. The older form of the confessional prayer of the Roman Church is to "almighty God, to blessed Mary ever virgin, to blessed Michael the Archangel, to blessed John the Baptist, to the holy Apostles Peter and Paul, etc." John outranks all human beings mentioned, except Mary. Another impressive bit of evidence is presented by Gottschald in *Deutsche Namenkunde* p. 60. Most of the St. John's churches in the Rhineland have John the Baptist as their patron saint, instead of John the Evangelist. In Bavaria they are 241 to 21, in the Köln diocese 64 to 16, Münster 21 to 3.[1] Protestantism discarded these relics of the prominence of the Baptist, and from the New Testament itself hardly suspects it, since five books are traditionally ascribed to John the Evangelist, and none to the Baptist, while Peter and Paul are the most prominent leaders. Acts 18:24-19:7 shows there was a Baptist movement in both Alexandria and Ephesus, but it must have been even more widespread.

Many have noticed the similarity of John the Baptist to Jewish monastics as pictured in statements of Philo, Pliny the Elder, and Josephus.[2] The Qumran discoveries make it seem even more possible that John was a member of some monastic order. Monastic ideas had more effect on developing Christianity than Protestants realize. Though almost never mentioned among Protestants, the example of Jesus has no doubt always been a powerful factor in Christian celibacy.

In Acts 19:8-10 we are told Paul began his Ephesian campaign by preaching for three months in a synagogue, but after contentions arose he withdrew to the school of Tyrannus, where he spoke daily for two years, so that his work became known throughout the province of Asia.

A popular field of religious superstition is mentioned here in Acts. People took aprons and handkerchiefs that Paul had touched to those who were sick, and they were cured, both of diseases and of evil spirits. Whether of pagan or Jewish prompting, it is one of the earliest notices of the use of relics by Chris-

---

[1] From *Festschrift to Honor F. Wilbur Gingrich*, p. 207. Leiden, 1972.
[2] Philo: De vita cont., passim; Quot omnis probus liber, 75; Hypothetica, 11.1-18; etc. Pliny: 5.17, etc. Josephus: Ant. 13.5.9; 15.10.4-5; etc.; War 2.82-13; etc.

tians. Acts 5:15 speaks of healings by even more tenuous contact. These passages are used by apologists of the old churches in support of the cult of relics today, and by some Protestants for similar practices. I have a personal letter from an American Protestant group claiming healing powers for anointed and blessed handkerchiefs.

Acts also tells of Jewish exorcists. A certain class of Jews were among the occult practicioners of the ancient Mediterranean world. There are numerous notices of such ministrations in the New Testament, as well as in contemporary pagan literature. Although the Synoptics report exorcisms, there are none in the Fourth Gospel.

A third item in this general picture of superstition is the burning of magic books told about in Acts 19:19. There are of course many magic books in various languages on the market today. Ephesus was noted as a center of such things in the ancient world.

During his Ephesian campaign Paul made some visits to Corinth and Macedonia, but the details are not clear. One of his main purposes was to raise a large sum of money to take back to Jerusalem. This would help heal the breach between the Palestinian Christians and those of the gentile world, a breach he perhaps had done more to cause than anyone else. But he was just as desirous of effecting a reconciliation as he had been to secure liberty to gentile converts. He speaks of this fund raising several times in his letters. Whether it accomplished its purpose is not known. There seems to have been a great deal of poverty among the Christians at Jerusalem. It was probably for this reason that they had at one time initiated a form of communism. An incident attending his delivery of the gift brought about his arrest, with the result that he spent the next five years of his life in prison, the last five as far as we know; first, two in Caesarea and then, after voyage and shipwreck, two at Rome.

3. GALATIANS

Consideration of Paul's letters as individual documents may well begin with Galatians, because it is possibly the earliest, throws more light on the chronology of his life than any other letter, and is the most crucial of all, containing the essence of his principles.

Galatians is primarily concerned with Paul's struggle to free Christians from literal adherence to Scripture. Now being in union with Christ they have real freedom. He says in 2:11 that after his second trip to Jerusalem he and Cephas had a sharp dispute at Antioch. Leviticus 11, etc., prescribe a limited diet, excluding a considerable number of animals. These dietary prohibitions are among the parts of the Bible to which Paul especially objected. Christians were to constitute a brotherhood, but brotherhood is difficult among those who cannot eat each other's cooking.

Since the first Christians were Jews they naturally regarded Judaism as the normal prelude to Christianity, as the path by which converts from paganism should come to faith in Jesus as the Anointed. Moses had been the attendant who had led these Jews to Christ. Why should not he also be the one to lead the heathen? As others saw it, dietary regulations and circumcision were proving serious hindrances to bringing non-Jews into the Church. Paul was determined to do away with these hindrances.

The highest religious and social ideals have some of their most effective expression in Galatians. The Christian society is to be classless. There is to be no distinction between Jew and heathen, slave and free, man and woman; but all are to be equal and united in Christ Jesus. Galatians 3:28 is a parody on part of a synagogue prayer known as the Eighteen Benedictions. The second, third, and fourth of these benedictons are: "Blessed art thou, O Lord our God, king of the universe, who hast not made me a heathen. Blessed art thou, O Lord our God, king of the universe, who hast not made me a slave. Blessed art thou, O Lord our God, king of the universe, who hast not made me a woman." For the last clause, according to modern prayer books, women substitute, "Who hast made me as I am." It is only fair to say that Reform Judaism has been as progressive as Christendom in abolishing such prejudices.

Paul himself failed to live up to the exalted ideal of his parody. He told the Romans, 3:2, that Jews have the advantage in every

38

way. He told the Christian slaves at Corinth, First Corinthians 7:20-21, not to try to gain their freedom; and he would not allow Corinthian women to say anything in church, First Corinthians 14:34-35.

It would be hard to find a finer list of ideal traits of character than the one in Galatians 5:22, "The fruits of the Spirit are love, joy, peace, patience, kindness, goodness, faithfulness, gentleness, and self-control." [1] Do we have here the spiritual portrait of Christ as painted by Paul?

The firm hold early Christianity had on the great commandment of Leviticus 19:18 is first attested by Galatians 5:14, "The whole Law is fulfilled in one saying, 'You must love your neighbor as yourself.'"

Christ had freed Paul from the belief that all Scripture is profitable. Like the writer of the Fourth Gospel he is convinced that no limitations of time or space are involved in acceptable worship. He would remove all ritualistic and material requirements. "It is for freedom that Christ set us free." Galatians 5:1. The essentials are all involved in the word love, mutual love among men, between God and man, and between man and Christ.

In the opening passages of the letter he attributes the reconstruction of his ideas largely to ecstatic experience. Though we may not believe such experiences contribute new elements to thought, yet they certainly crystallize new combinations and mark radical changes in many lives.

The distance that separates us from Paul's thought is strikingly illustrated in the fourth chapter where he speaks of the danger of his converts becoming enslaved to "weak and poverty-stricken ghosts," which are the rulers of this world. Elsewhere he refers to supernatural beings in the following language: "principality and authority and power," First Corinthians 15:24; "the god of this age," Second Corinthians 4:4; "ghosts of the world," Colossians 2:8, 20; "principalities and authorities," Colossians 2:15. Compare also Ephesians 1:21, 2:2, 6:12; Hebrews 12:22; First Peter 3:22; Revelation 7:1, 14:18, 16:5, 19:17.

---

[1] E. J. Goodspeed, *The New Testament, An American Translation*, Copyright 1923 by the University of Chicago.

Whatever the validity of ideas Paul attributed to ecstatic experience, it seems clear they were essential factors in his career, in the fusion of strenuous emotion and high ideals.

Though the letter is not intended as literature, it is great writing. Though Paul's Greek is colloquial, he is capable of striking eloquence.

Paul's second visit to Jerusalem and the Antioch scene must have marked the height of the dietary and circumcision controversies. Since Galatians is the most heated account, it may be inferred it is the earliest. One of the chief contrasts between Paul's letters and Acts is their different picture of these controversies. From both Galatians and Acts we learn there was disagreement in the early church over ritual commandments in the Bible, instructions that Orthodox Jews observe, but which most Christians regard as of only historical significance. Acts 15:22-29 represents Paul agreeing to a compromise on the whole question, but in Galatians 2:6 he says the Jerusalem leaders made no demand of him.

In Galatians 1:16-2:1 he says that after his conversion he went to Arabia and then returned to Damascus, and that three years later he went up to Jerusalem. He stayed only two weeks and then went to the districts of Syria and Cilicia, i.e., the regions near Antioch and Tarsus. Fourteen years later, at least seventeen years after his conversion, he went up to Jerusalem again. This second trip cannot be earlier than 44, for as stated above, his conversion cannot be earlier than 27. So we have 44 as the earliest possible date for Galatians.

Endless controversy has developed over the question whether Galatians was written during his second or third journey. It appears from Galatians 4:13 that Paul had visited Galatia twice, though a different interpretation of the Greek is possible. Did he visit Galatia on his first and second, or on his second and third journeys? It is not certain just what is meant by Galatia. Is it a Roman administrative division, or a region formerly having somewhat different boundaries? Leading authorities are found on each side of the question. The problem seems insoluble. So we do not know whether the letter is one of the earliest or one of the latest, i.e., around 49 or near 60.

Just where he went in Arabia, or what he did there, or how long he stayed, we do not know. Could his break with the Pharisees have been mediated by a visit among the Essenes or other Jewish monastics? His writings show traces of such influences.

At any rate, Galatians is a charter member of the New Testament, and its place in the canon has always been secure.

4. FIRST THESSALONIANS

The warmth of Paul's affection for this congregation is one of the chief impressions made by First Thessalonians. It is plain enough from the rest of his letters that he was a man of intense feeling. The great rhapsody of First Corinthians 13 shows what a fundamental place love had in his view of the Christian life. First Thessalonians is a love letter. He calls the congregation his "glory and joy," praising them for the example of faith and piety they have set before the rest of Greece.

In this letter he mentions his observance of the rabbinical principle that a religious teacher should engage in manual labor. Although he says in First Corinthians 9:3-18 that congregations should supply the material needs of their ministers, he himself prefers to be independent.

The bitter anti-Semitism in 2:15 is startling. As in the speeches in Acts, the blunt accusation is made that "the Jews killed the Lord Jesus." The Synoptic Gospels plainly state that the Romans executed him, though they say with equal clarity that some of his own people denounced him before the Roman authorities. Paul never states the Roman arrest, trial, condemnation, and execution. In Acts 16:37 and 22:25 it is stated that, sometimes at least, he relied on his Roman citizenship to protect him from persecution. In Romans 13:1-7 he strongly urges loyalty to the civil government, and always seems careful to say nothing against the Roman power. The attack against the Jews in this passage may have sprung from some recent violence offered him by those who rejected his gospel. Possibly there is some connexion between the outburst and the trouble referred to in the opening lines of the letter.

The congregation at Thessalonica was largely composed of former pagans, for he reminds them that they had turned from idols to serve the living God. Jews were not idolaters. Pagans called them atheists because they had no visible gods.

Not only were the Thessalonians serving the living and true God, but they were expecting the coming of his son from heaven. It is hard for most of us to realize how vividly the early Christians expected the return of the glorified Jesus in their own day. Passages in Paul's letters and the Synoptic Gospels show they were expecting the return of the Anointed any minute. According to the Synoptics Jesus had promised to return while some of his hearers were still living. Now, twenty years or so later, Paul had taught the Thessalonians that the time was surely drawing near.

The best known passage in First Thessalonians is 4:13-18, which is universally used at Christian funerals, "I don't want you to be uninformed, brothers, about those who are asleep, etc."

Paul's letters are first doctrinal, then ethical. The former rabbi never lost his interest in morals, and insisted that his converts be holy, blameless, never returning evil for evil, patient with all. In Thessalonica as elsewhere he found it necessary to condemn gentile standards of sex relations, which were so far below the Jewish. He also feels he must urge upon them the virtue of hospitality, loving fellowship, and industry.

The ceremonial kiss, which has had such a long and curious tradition, is here prescribed. In one of its modern forms it is equivalent to throwing a kiss.

There is another prescription of greater consequence, viz., "I adjure you by the Lord that this letter be read to all the brothers." This may be the first instance of the Epistle Lesson, a regular feature in most Christian public worship.

First Thessalonians is regarded by most students as the earliest of Paul's extant letters. The fact that it comes before Second Thessalonians in the New Testament does not prove that it was written first, since Paul's letters are arranged according to length rather than dates. But when the two letters are read in succession one gets the impression that they stand in their chronological order. The first seems like an introductory document and makes no mention of previous writing. The second seems to be re-emphasizing certain points and refers to previous communication.

The closing clause of 2:16 is startling. It can hardly refer to anything but the destruction of Jerusalem in the year 70. It sounds like a reader's note that was later incorporated into the text.

The letter itself must have been written in the year 50. It is the only New Testament book for which a date is so sure. According to Acts 18:11 Paul stayed in Corinth a year and a half before the usual violence began, causing him to be haled into the court of Gallio, the Roman proconsul of Achaea. Proconsuls usually held office for one year. The reasonable inference is that as soon as the new proconsul arrived, the Jewish congregation, hoping for a change of policy, attempted legal action against Paul. Adolph Deissman in Appendix I of his book *Paul*, discusses the whole situation and archeological evidence in careful detail.

Fragments of a Roman imperial inscription fixing the date have been discovered at Delphi, which was in the province of Achaea. These fragments show the date of Gallio's term of office. It seems he became proconsul in June of 51. This would place Paul's arrival early in 50. He must have written to the Thessalonians soon after his arrival, and another letter not much later.

5. SECOND THESSALONIANS

The purpose of this letter is to correct some of the ideas held by the Thessalonians about the second coming. Since they could not know the date, they must not stop their regular work. Besides, "the man of lawlessness" must precede the coming of the Christ. As the Seleucid emperor, Antiochus Epiphanes, in the second century B.C. became the abomination of desolation by attacking the Jewish faith and profaning the Temple, so must another man of lawlessness arise to profane the Temple and defy all that is holy. This was to happen before the rev-

43

elation of the Lord Jesus from heaven, when he comes with all his angels in a flame of fire bringing destruction to all his adversaries.

In spite of Paul's stern warning that they should continue their usual occupations until the actual arrival, there have been from that time to this those who thought they could set the date and have actually quit work in order to be perfectly ready. It was for such folks that Paul gave the order that if they would not work they should not be fed, a bit of New Testament that got into the Russian constitution.

Those who make a hobby of the second coming naturally make much use of both letters to the Thessalonians.

The two letters have much in common, so much so that the authenticity of Second Thessalonians has been questioned. However, aside from the similar theme, there seems little reason to doubt its authorship, except that it contains Paul's only reference to "the man of lawlessness." The two objections cancel. A suspicious reader may feel that 2:2 and 3:17 betray a forger's anxiety. At least 2:2 shows he had the possibility of forgery in mind. If either letter is a forgery, it must be an early one. Both use the colloquial language of Paul's usual level. Then there is the simple benediction and the use of the early word Satan. The term used to designate the prince of evil is one of the straws in the wind giving indication of dates of New Testament books. First and Second Thessalonians, First and Second Corinthians, Romans, and Mark use only the Hebrew word Satan. Matthew, Luke, John, Acts, Revelation, and First Timothy use both Satan and the Greek word devil. Ephesians, Second Timothy, Titus, Hebrews, First Peter, First John, and Jude use only devil. This corresponds to the relative dates scholars have assigned these three groups on entirely other grounds.

6. FIRST CORINTHIANS

After the usual thanksgiving, First Corinthians takes up a series of problems that have arisen in the church at Corinth. As a result this letter is our best source for the nature of gentile Christianity in the middle of the first century.

Paul deplores the dawn of denominationalism at Corinth, points out the humble station of Christians there, reminds them he is an evangelist rather than a pastor, warns against the development of jealousy and selfish rivalry, prescribes excommunication for certain sex offenders, advises putting up with injustice rather than going to law in heathen courts, advocates celibacy, partly in view of the Lord's imminent coming, but partly due to the strong monastic strain Christianity showed from the first. He gives advice on marriage relations, partly from oral tradition, partly from his own judgment.

In contrast to the ideal of a classless society expressed in Galatians 3:28, he argues for patriarchal authority in the family, and for silence on the part of women in church.

Although quoting the oral tradition that the Lord forbade divorce, he permits separation without remarriage. If one of the faithful had an unbelieving spouse, the marriage was to be continued if the unbeliever was willing; but if the unbeliever wanted to separate, the believer was to let him go.

Paul states emphatically that the effect of a pagan ritual is purely imaginary, but advocates a curb on personal liberty whenever it might injure an overscrupulous person, i.e., the golden rule is to be tempered with sympathetic thoughtfulness, the sensitive consideration of the trials and needs of others. He demands that members of the Christian Church sever their connexion with pagan faiths.

He argues that ministers have a right to a living from the Church, though he himself prefers not to exercise the right. He also has the right to take a wife around with him, just as Jesus' brothers and Cephas do. In this connexion he reminds them that he has seen the Lord, and so does not lack this qualification of apostleship.

There are suggestions of Plato in this letter. They must be evidence of popular sayings in the Greek world, rather than of any acquaintance Paul himself had with the text of Plato. First Corinthians 6:7 suggests the Socratic principle of Gorgias 474 B, etc., that it is better to be injured than to injure. The statement in 8:2, "If a man thinks he knows something, he does not know as well as he ought," is a neat summary of Socrates' account in the Apology, 21 A-23 B, of how his friend was told by the oracle at Delphi that no one was wiser than Socrates, and how Socrates could not accept this till it occurred to him that he was the only person who realized his own ignorance. The athletic reference in First Corinthians 9:25 might be compared to Laws 840 B, but was no doubt an obvious figure for any ancient Greek moralist, athletics being so prominent in Greek life.

Paul often interprets Old Testament passages figuratively, but in 10:4 goes further and allegorizes from a Jewish legend about a rock that followed Israel in the desert.

Ancient Jews and Christians believed that angels attended religious services along with mortals. This is obviously what 11:10 refers to. Attractive coiffures might divert angels from their business, which was to carry the prayers to God.[3] The restriction of the passage must be a device for keeping women under control.

First Corinthians 11:23 ff. is the earliest account of the Last Supper, beginning with the words, "The Lord Jesus, the night he was betrayed, took bread, etc." After the words of institution the account shifts to the third person, i.e., Paul pieces out the tradition with his own views.

It should be especially noted that he does not say the Last Supper was the Passover meal (Seder), in spite of the Synoptic tradition to that effect. Paul implies and the Fourth Gospel states that Jesus was crucified before the Seder. The Last Supper may have been just a usual evening meal. Paul was not concerned with such questions. The fact that it was the last meal of Jesus with his disciples was what made it sacred for him. Later developments in its celebration were influenced by the Seder, by pagan sacraments, and possibly by Jewish monastic practices.

The statement in 11:30 that many had gotten sick and some had died because of unfitting behavior at communion makes it plain that Paul believed a supernatural power was present at the meal. His attitude here seems a forerunner of stories of miracle working hosts as told by Cyprian in Treatise 3.25-26, and by

---

[3] For citation of authorities see Renan, *Saint Paul,* p. 402, Paris 1899.

later writers, e.g., Kyriakos in his modern novel *Kassiané,* and still believed by the majority of Christians.

We are reminded in First Corinthians that other religions had communion rituals. Some of the competitors of early Christianity, i.e., cults with a secret ritual—some of these had communion services. Justin Martyr, in Apology 66, written a century later than Paul, explains the close resemblance of Christian and Mithraic communions by claiming that "the wicked demons of Mithra had spied on" the Christian sacrament and taught the Mithra initiates to imitate it. He no doubt had cause and effect reversed. Christian converts who had been Mithraites had brought ideas with them into the Church. Cyprian in Epistle 62.2, writing a century later than Justin, seems to show that some Christians were still imitating the Mithra liturgy, since they were using water instead of wine in the communion. And what about the warning in First John that Christ came not with water only, but with water and blood? Today most of the Christians in the world mix water with wine in the communion. Could this be the result of an ancient compromise? Gentile converts brought more or less paganism into the Church. Paul warns them in 10:21 that they cannot drink the cup of the Lord and the cup of demons.

In further discussion of worship, 14:26-40, he advocates rigid control of ecstatic speaking, and outlines what he considers a model program for a Christian meeting. It closely resembles an enthusiastic Protestant prayer meeting.

In 12:1-3 there is a strange parenthetical statement that "no one is able to say Jesus is Lord, except by the Holy Spirit." This statement immediately follows the words, "No one speaking in God's spirit says Jesus is accursed." A half century later Pliny the Younger, writing to Trajan in Letters x.96 (97), says no Christian could be forced to revile Christ.

The Corinthian church was having trouble with the rivalries and jealousies of church officers and, no doubt, with some unqualified persons who wanted to be officers. In chapter 12, one of the best known passages, Paul reminds them of the various functions required in a church, and of the varying abilities of church members. He considers church officers to be of divine

47

appointment. His list of officers deserves special attention. The main kinds are apostles, prophets, and teachers. The traditional orders of bishop, priest, and deacon had not yet developed in this third decade of Christianity. He also lists such secondary functionaries as wonder workers, healers, helpers, administrators, and ecstatic speakers. Suddenly he rises to his highest eloquence as he tells the Corinthian congregation in chapter 13 that the general solvent for all its difficulties is love. We cannot begin to understand Paul unless we realize the supreme place love had in his scheme of Christian virtues.

Equally important is his statement of what he means by the "good news." This passage, 15:2-8, contains nuclei of the creeds that developed during the following centuries, particularly the Apostles' and Nicene. The oral tradition as Paul had received it and as he had passed it on to the Corinthians was "Christ died for our sins according to the Scriptures; he was buried, and on the third day was raised again according to the Scriptures; he appeared to Cephas, then to the twelve, then to more than five hundred brothers all at once, most of whom are still living, though some have died; next he appeared to James, then to all the apostles, and last of all, as to an abortion, he appeared to me." This passage is our earliest account of the resurrection. As in the specimen of oral tradition on the Last Supper, the beginning of the quotation is sharply marked, while the last clause is what Paul added. It is the growing tip. This oral tradition was the good news as Paul defines it in this chapter.

Another important matter grows directly out of this version of the good news, viz., the belief in the resurrection of all Christians. As Christ was raised, so will all his people be raised. His resurrection is the guarantee of theirs. His resurrection was the "first fruits," an allusion to the second day of Passover, when the first sheaf of newly harvested grain was waved as an offering. Without the resurrection the whole Christian movement is meaningless and futile. Paul agrees that the Pharisaic idea of the resurrection of the body is hard to understand. It may be illustrated by the planting of an inert seed and watching the plant grow. To Corinthians the symbol of the sprouting grain was a reminder of the mysteries celebrated annually at Eleusis, a short distance to the west. Eleusis was one of the most famous shrines of the ancient world, an object of patronage even for Roman emperors. In the Eleusinian rites sprouting grain was a symbol of resurrection. Paul says the resurrection body will be a different body, for "flesh and blood cannot inherit the kingdom of God." This statement undoubtedly furnished aid and comfort to Docetists, and embarrassment to orthodox Christians in years to follow. Docetism was the heresy that taught Jesus had no real flesh and blood human body, and only seemed to be a man "of like passions with us."

Paul expected the general resurrection to take place when the Lord returned, which was to be soon, while some of his own generation were still living. In First Thessalonians 4:17 he says, "Those of us who are still alive will be caught up into the air." At this moment the natural body was to be miraculously changed into a glorious "spiritual body."

The remainder of the letter discusses plans for the collection to be taken for the poor at Jerusalem; states his plan to visit Macedonia and Corinth again and to wait at Ephesus till Pentecost; includes a recommendation of Timothy; promises a visit of Apollos; urges cooperation with the leadership of the household of Stephanas; and extends certain greetings. Following his signature is a curse on those who do not love the Lord, then the Aramaic cult cry, *maran atha* (our Lord is coming), and finally a benediction.

Paul's extant Corinthian correspondence was written from Ephesus, where he spent a large part of the third journey. It must have been in the middle fifties. From our First Corinthians 5:9 we learn that he had written to Corinth before. Whether we have this former letter is a question. Paul's letters are arranged in the New Testament according to their length. First Corinthians comes before Second Corinthians because it is longer, not because it was written earlier. We cannot be sure whether the letter referred to in First Corinthians 5:9 is our Second Corinthians or some lost letter. The problem will be discussed further in connexion with Second Corinthians.

It seems likely that Paul wrote at least four letters to the church at Corinth, viz.,

1. A lost letter
2. Our First Corinthians
3. A severe letter
4. A conciliatory letter

Second Corinthians gives a certain impression of disconnectedness. This may be due to Paul's impetuosity. He dictated his letters, at least some of them. Sometimes his thoughts seem to have gotten so far ahead of the writing that the gaps were never closed. The sharp breaks in Second Corinthians have led some to the view that the book as it now stands is a combination of two or three letters. We do not know how many letters he wrote to Corinth. First Corinthians 5:9, Second Corinthians 7:8 and 10:9-11 speak of former letters. The second reference is to a letter that hurt their feelings. This is hardly our First Corinthians, though it does contain some reprimands. The last four chapters of Second Corinthians have sharp criticisms and may be the severe letter. Assuming this is so, we note the severe letter, 10:9-11, mentions former letters; so the severe letter would be at least the third, and is itself mentioned in a later letter. So if the last four chapters of Second Corinthians are the severe letter, then he wrote at least four letters to Corinth. There seems little doubt that the severe letter either is lost or is the last four chapters of Second Corinthians.

In attempting to reconstruct the probable order of his Corinthian correspondence we are sure of three things: the severe letter was written before the first part of Second Corinthians; more than one letter was written before the severe letter; and our First Corinthians was not the first. The conciliatory letter would then be at least the fourth.

THE SEVERE LETTER (10-13)

If the above reconstruction is correct, we should take up these last four chapters before the rest of the book.

The best known passage is the list of sufferings: "Are they Christ's ministers? This is insane talk. I am a better one. I have worked harder, been imprisoned more, been beaten excessively, often at the point of death, Jews whipped me five times with thirty-nine stripes, three times I was beaten with a rod, once I was stoned, thrice shipwrecked, spent a night and a day in the deep, made many journeys, risked dangers in rivers, dangers of bandits, dangers from my own people, dangers from gentiles, dangers in the city, dangers in the desert, dangers in the sea, dangers from false brothers, in labor and weariness, spent many sleepless nights, underwent hunger and thirst, endured many fasts, cold and nakedness. Beside all that, my constant care, the worry about all the churches. Who is sick without my being sick? Who stumbles without my burning? If I must boast, I will boast about my infirmities." (11:21b-31)

He is most autobiographical when engaged in passionate self-defense.

He seems to have worked in a given field till violent opposition began. This letter tells of his flight from Damascus under such circumstances. He also makes it clear that he was the victim of some chronic affliction, but there is no indication of its nature. The usual speculations are hardly worth mentioning.

The severity of the letter clearly enough was occasioned by certain would-be leaders of the church at Corinth, who used denunciation of Paul as one means of gaining control. This would involve opposition to some of his teachings. It is plain from Galatians that such opposition was the one thing he would not tolerate.

An important biographical item is the report of a supremely glorious vision he had had fourteen years earlier, 12:1-4. That must have been some ten years after his conversion experience on the way to Damascus. The year 54 seems a fair estimate of the date of the severe letter. He was on the eve of a third visit to Corinth. Whether he carried out the plan we do not know.

THE CONCILIATORY LETTER (1-9)

These chapters are dominated by an extended appeal for additional contributions to the fund being raised for the relief of the Jerusalem church. The matter is urgent and presented with impressive diplomacy, involving some of the most beloved quotations current among evangelical Christians, such as: "But we all with uncovered face, reflecting the glory of the Lord, are changed into the same form from glory to glory," 3:18. "The illumination of the good news of Christ's glory," 4:4. "Visible things are temporary, but invisible things are eternal," 4:18. "For I know that if the tent of our earthly dwelling is destroyed, we have in the heavens an eternal building from God, one not made with hands," 5:1. "If anyone is in union with Christ he is a new creation," 5:17. "Godly sorrow produces repentance, leading to a healing that will never be regretted," 7:10. "They first gave themselves to the Lord," 8:5. "Thank God for his inexpressible gift," 9:15. "The letter kills, but the spirit gives life," 3:6.

8. ROMANS

Anxious to prepare a favorable opening for his evangelical activity in the Empire's capital city, as well as to set before them clearly some of his own ideas, he wrote this letter to the remarkable congregation of Christians already in existence at Rome in the fourth decade of the Christian movement. The letter became the head of the Pauline corpus because of its length, but its weight and destination make the position appropriate.

Careful to state his own authority and mission in a monumental opening sentence, he goes on immediately to express his admiration and loving concern for the church at Rome, his longing to see them, and his intention to come and work among them, so that he can share the glorious good news.

If it is predominantly a doctrinal treatise, it is doctrine aflame with vehement and indomitable love for Christ. The depraved and hopeless condition of the unevangelized world is pictured in language that has become classic among Christians. Both Jew and gentile are in utter need. Jesus Christ is the all-sufficient redeemer, both for time and eternity. The quibble of those who suggest that faith in Christ relieves them of personal responsibility is emphatically rejected. Paul's mortal grief over the fact that Jews as a group have not accepted the good news is partly comforted by the reflection that the true Israel is not formed physically, but spiritually, a reminder of the statement of Isocrates, written over four centuries earlier, that "A Greek is not one who is born such, but one who has shared in Greek civilization," Panegyricus 50.

The problem of evil, as it appears in the case of those whom God has not predestined to become his children, is not solved, but silenced by an appeal to God's absolute sovereignty.

Following the theological portion, which constitutes the bulk of the letter, is one of the finest of all early Christian synopses of ethical exhortation. The twelfth chapter of Romans is second only to the Sermon on the Mount as an outline of ideal behavior.

After the ethical portion Paul again states that, being now on the way back to Jerusalem, at the end of his journey, he plans next to go to Spain by way of Rome. Whether he is writing from Ephesus, Corinth, or Macedonia is not certain. The great Ephesian mission, as some others, had come to a violent close. The riot about Artemis is Act's version, 19:23-41. Paul himself says in First Corinthians 15:32 that he had been in deadly danger in Ephesus. It seems he must have written to the Romans after this, while paying farewell visits to communities to the north and west of the Aegean. It must have been near the year 60.

The original close of the letter seems to have been the end of chapter 15. Whether 16 is a postcript or another letter is not certain. It seems possible to regard it as a note from Corinth to Ephesus. In any case it shows the mixed character of early Christian names, all Latin and Greek except one from Hebrew, but even Maria is in Greek form.

It must have been during this third journey that he visited Illyricum, but we know nothing about it except the bare statement in Romans 15:19. He no doubt went by the Egnatian Road, which led through Thessalonica and Edessa, and which he must have travelled from Neapolis to Philippi and on west on his second journey.

The second we section, Acts 20:5-16, begins when the writer joins Paul's party at Troas. The year must have been between 55 and 60. If Paul first arrived in Corinth in 50, and stayed a year and a half, and we may add another year for the return to Antioch and the trip back to Ephesus, followed by two years in Ephesus and some time in Macedonia and Illyricum, the barest minimum for all this is five years.

Acts 20:17-25 emphasizes Paul's premonition of martyrdom, especially in verse 25 where he tells the Ephesian elders he knows he will never see them again. This item is likely included because his martyrdom had occurred by the time Acts was written.

The fact that the third we section, 21:1-25, ends with Paul's arrival at Caesarea, and that the fourth, 27:1-28:16, does not begin till two years later when Paul started for Rome, tempts the suggestion that Luke spent the intervening time collecting materials for his Gospel and Acts.

According to Acts, when Paul finally arrived at Jerusalem with the collection, he was advised to further placate the Jewish party by paying the expenses of some young men for a rite they were completing at the Temple. Paul's presence at the Temple was misunderstood and a disturbance developed that resulted in his being taken into custody by the Romans. The delays of courts controlled by politicians prolonged his imprisonment for two years. Finally in desperation he appealed to Caesar. The trip to Rome, with its dramatic account of the shipwreck and getting to land at Malta, occupies most of the fourth we section. The last part of the last chapter tells how Paul spent two years as a prisoner at Rome, a sort of trusty, living in his own rented quarters and engaging in missionary work.

The failure of Acts to tell anything about Paul's death is one of the unsolved problems. If we could believe Acts was completed before his death it would make an easy solution; but it would push the composition of the Gospel back too far. One wonders whether there could have been something inglorious about Paul's death that caused it not to be recorded.

Certainly there is much about his career that we do not know. Acts tells of a shipwreck, but in Second Corinthians we learn there were three before that. Much else in the list of sufferings shows we have only glimpses of his life and travels. It seems clear also that the writer of Acts did not have access to a collection of Paul's letters.

For further information on his Roman imprisonment one must search his letters of that period. These are assumed to be Philippians, Colossians, and Philemon.

10. PHILIPPIANS

There is something especially fine about the tone of this letter. The Christian graces of "love, joy, peace, patience, kindness, goodness, faithfulness, gentleness, and self-control" are in full flower in the character of the veteran missionary as he faces a death sentence in the court of Nero. In this situation he is able to say, "I have learned, in whatever circumstances I am, to be self-sufficient," 4:11.

There is evidence of development in his Christology. Christ Jesus had existed in God's form, but gave up this power and honor temporarily and assumed the nature of a slave, 2:6-7. As a reward for this humility God exalted him most highly, bestowing on him the name that is above every name, so that every knee in the universe would bow before him, and every tongue acknowledge his lordship. In this ascription Paul borrows language applied to God in Isaiah 45:23, where the strictest monotheism is proclaimed. Nowhere else does Paul ascribe actual deity to Christ so plainly, unless in Romans 9:5.

In Philippians 3:4-7 he makes a strong statement of his Jewish heritage, both physical and cultural. It is a common tendency of converts to emphasize the nature of their former state so the contrast will show the power and glory of their conversion, which is what he is doing in this passage.

In closing he mentions Euodia, Syntyche, and Clement as fellow-workers, and thanks the people at Philippi for the financial assistance they have given him time and again, including this last gift sent by the hand of Epaphroditus. He must have enjoyed the ironical pun in his plea to Euodia (**bon voyage**, fragrance) and Syntyche (coincidence) that they agree with one another.

The letter is from both Paul and Timothy. Paul is a prisoner. From his mention of the imperial guard and imperial household it is usually assumed that the letter was written from Rome. His imprisonment has been good advertisement for the new faith. He is sending Epaphroditus, who we may assume was the bearer of the letter.

11. Colossians

This letter is a warning against Neoplatonism and certain early forms of Gnosticism. Believing matter to be essentially evil, they thought the supreme deity must be too holy to have any contact with the material world. A mythology was developed to explain how the perfectly holy supreme being could have been the cause of a physical universe. According to this theosophy there came from the supreme being a series of emanations called eons. The first eon produced a second, the second a third, and so on until finally an eon was produced sufficiently remote from the first cause to be capable of dealing with matter. This last eon was the immediate cause in the creation of the world.

Paul uses some of the Gnostic language to explain his own concept of creation. For him Christ takes the place of the whole chain of eons, and is the acting agent in the creation of all things. This same view was expressed forty or fifty years later by the author of the Fourth Gospel, and finally became the standard Christian dogma. The necessity, as Paul saw it, of correcting Gnostic speculation was no doubt a factor in the development of his own thinking. Similar motives caused further development in later centuries. Christian leaders were constantly correcting views that seemed to them essentially alien. The development of orthodoxy was largely a reaction to heresy.

In this letter Paul shows himself to be the earliest known advocate of the idea that a pre-existent divine being, who had existed before all creation, and through whose agency all things had been created, had taken on human nature and become incarnate in Jesus, 1:13-17. In this connexion he also explicitly states that God's son had redeemed all the faithful from their sins. In the light of these clear statements on incarnation and atonement it seems that Paul, instead of John the Evangelist, deserves the title theologian. The developed Christology of the prison letters has led some to doubt their genuiness, but Paul's was not a static mind. It seems reasonable to suppose there was continual development in his religious ideas as long as he lived.

His opposition to the theosophy encountered by the Colossians reveals something of his own ideas about a hierarchy of angels. No doubt many readers of 2:10 assume the "governments and authorities" mentioned there to be civil institutions of this world, but the more elaborate wording of Ephesians 1:21 makes it clear that the words refer to supernatural beings.

When in 2:16f. he denounces all ritual observances, one wonders whether he has in mind the teachings of Amos, Hosea, Isaiah, Micah, etc. He was of course familiar with the prophets.

Colossians contains the earliest Christian summary of mutual household obligations between husbands and wives, parents and children, masters and slaves, 3:18-4:1, which along with much else is paralleled or borrowed by Ephesians and First Peter.

Paul says he is having a hard struggle in behalf of the Colossians and Laodiceans, but rejoices because of the attendant sufferings. This sounds as if his imprisonment was in some way connected with these congregations. It has led some to suppose the imprisonment was at Ephesus. The fact that Aristarchus was a fellow prisoner lends weight to the view. Mark, Barnabas' cousin, is there with him, and may go to Colossae. Jesus, whose Roman name is Justus, is also with him. They are the only converts from Judaism who have cooperated with him. This is easy to understand, for Paul was considerably left of center. He also has a good friend Luke, a physician, who is in contact with him, and a man named Demas. These two join in sending greetings.

Paul and Timothy are still together. The letter opens with a joint salutation from Timothy. Epaphras, founder of the church at Colossae, has been the messenger to Paul. Paul's reply is to be sent with Tychicus and Onesimus, the latter likely Archippus' slave. In Philemon Paul asks to have Onesimus freed to help him in his work. It seems Paul had never been to Colossae, but has been praying for them ever since he first heard of the congregation.

He has some special Christian service in mind that he wants Archippus to perform, and seems to have some doubt whether he will comply. He asks the congregation to remind Archippus.

12. PHILEMON

This letter should be considered with Colossians, for it was sent at the same time and is intimately related. It may be the letter to the Laodiceans that is mentioned at the end of Colossians. It is from Paul and Timothy to Philemon their fellow worker, and Apphia the sister, and Archippus their fellow soldier, and the church that met in his house. Literal translations into English obscure the fact that the house belonged to Archippus.

The letter concerns Onesimus, whose spiritual father Paul has become while in prison. Paul would like to keep Onesimus with him, but is sending him back to his owner with a most diplomatically worded request that the master free Onesimus for the Christian ministry. Professor John Knox has published an impressive argument that Archippus was the owner, that he did comply with Paul's request, and that Onesimus eventually became bishop of Ephesus.[4]

When freed from the ridiculous archaisms of the King James version the irresistibly diplomatic appeal of the letter is much more obvious. The effectiveness is heightened by the pun on the name Onesimus (profitable), 11, 12, 20, "I am sending profit able back to you, who was formerly unprofitable to you, but now is profitable both to you and me . . . yes, brother, I would like to make some profit on you."

13. THE END OF PAUL'S LIFE

Primary sources end with Philemon. Acts ends with the statement that Paul was a prisoner at Rome for two years, living in

------

[4] *Philemon Among the Letters of Paul,* Chicago, 1935.

his own rented place. We cannot be certain whether he suffered martyrdom at the end of these two years, or was acquitted and released, and so enabled to visit Spain as he had planned. Clement of Rome, our earliest witness outside the New Testament, may be interpreted either way. In 5.7 he writes of Paul carrying his work to the "limits of the west." Does this mean Spain? Writing thirty years after Paul's death, Clement may not have been clear in his own mind.

The problem is intimately connected with the authenticity of the Pastoral Epistles, First and Second Timothy and Titus. If Second Timothy is taken at face value, we are to understand that at Paul's first trial everyone deserted him, but that the Lord stood by him strengthening him, and he was "saved from the lion's mouth." As far as we know, such an outcome of the trial would have enabled him to carry out his plan of visiting Spain. However, just before this passage, he announces his own martyrdom.

Clement, with the tantalizing indefiniteness of many early sources says, "Out of jealousy and conflict, Paul validated an endurance prize: seven times in chains, fugitive, stoned, preaching both in east and west, he won the noble fame due his faith, and after teaching righteousness in the whole world, and reaching the limits of the west, and testifying before the authorities, was released from the world and went to the place of holiness, after the greatest demonstration of steadfastness," 5.5-7. This passage is in the midst of a section dealing with martyrs, and immediately following a statement that Peter "on account of unjust jealousy had undergone not one, but many labors, and having witnessed had departed to the place of glory." It all plainly implies that Paul suffered martyrdom. The account continues with mention of a great crowd of the elect who had undergone many mistreatments, "women who as Danaids and Dirces had suffered fearful and unholy torments." In classical mythology the Danaids were condemned to carry water in sieves eternally. Dirce was tied to the horns of a wild bull.

Tacitus, Annals 15.44, is our earliest external authority for sufferings of Christians under Nero. It was not technically a persecution, for they were suffering merely as scapegoats for

Nero, who was trying to divert the blame from himself for the devastating fire that had just occurred. However, it seems quite possible some legal excuse was found for regarding Christians as violators of the law. In Annals 14.17.4 Tacitus says clubs at Pompeii were suppressed by Nero. There are also wall scribblings at Pompeii showing there were Christians there.

Tertullian in the fifth chapter of his Apology says Nero was the first to attack Christians with the imperial sword. He mentions Domitian next in the line of persecutors. Eusebius, a careful historian, writing in the fourth century, says in his Church History 2.25 that Gaius in a written discourse with Proclus, leader of the Montanists, at the beginning of the third century, says he can point out the trophies of the apostles, "for if you will go to the Vatican, or the Ostian Way, you will find the trophies of those who founded this church." Eusebius quotes Dionysius, bishop of Corinth in the latter part of the second century, whom he calls "one of the ancients," to the effect that Paul suffered martyrdom at the same time as Peter. Eusebius also states, Church History 2.25.5, without giving his authority, that Paul was beheaded. The foregoing are our earliest sources. The conjecture was made early that Paul would have availed himself of his Roman citizenship to avoid crucifixion. Use of his citizenship to gain immunities is attested only in Acts 16:37 and 22:25. It has been charged that he was a collaborationist. His exhortation to the Roman congregation to be loyal to the established government is his own most striking testimony on this point, 13:1. This attitude may have been a factor in his persecution by Jews. Could it have been a factor in his conversion?

Although Jews hated Paul for his defection, and though he too was embittered by the ordeal, we must not forget that Christianity is a development from Judaism. Even the Fourth Gospel, with all its alienation, recognizes that Christianity originated in Judaism and says, 4:22, "Salvation is from the Jews." This is true, however much evolution and accretion we may see in it. For their faith Christians have Judaism to thank, not blame.

Protestants are apt to forget that Luther and Calvin got their Christianity in and through the Roman Catholic Church, so

Christians generally are blind to the fact that Paul got his religion from Jews. However, we know that Judaism outside Palestine had been subject to strong gentile influences. The Hellenistic Judaism of Paul's day was not the purged orthodoxy of a few centuries later. Some of the Hellenistic features of Christianity came through the diaspora synagogue.

Protestants are also prone to forget that Paul was somewhat of a Catholic. Practically all modern Christians seek justification for their views in his writings, though the liberals in the major Protestant bodies are slow to work this mine. They should see that Paul too carried water on both shoulders, boldly setting aside certain large sections of the Bible while claiming the highest authority for the rest. Let it be fully recognized that Luther's great inspirational moment came while reading Romans, that there is no better immersionist text than Colossians 2:12, and that the Quaker type of meeting is described in First Corinthians 14:26-33. Nevertheless Paul probably would feel more at home in a Roman Catholic church today than in most Protestant churches, and still more at home in the Greek Orthodox Church, where his writings are still read in their original language. Paul is more alien to Protestantism than to the general milieu of sacramentalism and pre-scientific thinking found in all pre-Reformation groups, i.e., Roman Catholic, Eastern Orthodox, Armenian, Coptic, Nestorian, etc.

The outstanding marks of catholic tradition are the deification of Jesus, supernatural views of the sacraments, monarchial government, regarding celibacy as a preferable and holier state, and the practice of making huge blocks of Scripture acceptable by figurative and traditional interpretation. In all these attitudes Paul belongs with the Old Churches rather than with twentieth century Protestantism.

CHAPTER III

The Gospel, Oral and Written

1. THE ORAL GOSPEL

About forty years intervened between the death of Jesus and the writing of our oldest Gospel, the one according to Mark. As Abbé Ernest Dimnet reflected, there was a Christian belief before there was a Christian literature, *My Old World,* p. 199. Thus he reassured himself when disturbed by the havoc modern historical method had wrought in its investigation of traditional views of the Gospels. The fact is that Christianity produced the New Testament. The New Testament did not produce Christianity. Protestantism has suffered from an illusion to the contrary, for the New Testament was a chief factor in the formation of Protestantism. The New Testament itself is the product of the thought, feelings, and struggles of Christians during the first three centuries of the movement.

At first the new faith depended on oral tradition that was continually developing, and that differed in different localities. The principal factors operating to shape this oral tradition were: (1) the passion of Jesus, (2) the words and deeds of Jesus, (3) the spirit of Jesus, (4) the Septuagint, (5) the religious needs of the Christian communities.

The passion narratives were the first areas of gospel material to become standardized. This is shown by the fact that our canonical Gospels parallel one another more closely here than elsewhere. The principal interest of Christianity during the first century was in those parts of the gospel later embodied in the

Apostles' Creed. Compare First Corinthians 15. Interest in the miracles came next perhaps, with the words of Jesus ranking third. There was comparatively little interest in his earthly life, as shown by our canonical Gospels ignoring most of it and by Paul discounting it, Second Corinthians 5:16.

The words of Jesus are an indeterminate quantity. He undoubtedly used Aramaic, his mother tongue, more or less exclusively. The oral traditions of his Aramaic words were written down in Greek years later. In some instances a literal translation of his Aramaic words may have been preserved; but as Paul wrote in Second Corinthians 3:6, "The letter kills, the spirit gives life." The spirit was the highly prized endowment in early Christianity. Exact words were not so highly regarded. Consider Luke's version of the Our Father, 11:2-4, viz.:

> *Father, let your name be hallowed;*
> *Let your kingdom come;*
> *Give us each day our ration of bread;*
> *And forgive our sins,*
> *For indeed we forgive every one indebted to us;*
> *And do not lead us into temptation.*

Christians use the form given in Matthew 6:9-13.

Matthew's parable of the talents, 25:14-30, appears in Luke 19:12-27, as a parable of minas. In Matthew there are three slaves, one is given five talents, one two, and one one. When the master returned he found the first two had doubled their money, but the third had buried his. In Luke there are ten slaves, each given a mina. The first slave earned ten more with his, the second five, the third hid his away in a napkin; nothing is said about the other seven slaves.

We can hardly doubt that Jesus used parables, but how much they were modified and developed in transmission is forever impossible to know.

A few stray bits of the oral tradition of his sayings that did not get into the Gospels are found in other early Christian writings, e.g., Acts 20:35, "Remember the words of the Lord Jesus, that he said, 'It is more blessed to give than to receive.' " The same formula is used twice in First Clement, 13.1, "remembering the words of the Lord Jesus which he spoke . . . for he said the following: 'Have mercy so you may be shown mercy, forgive so you may be forgiven; as you do, so will it be done to you; as you give, so will it be given to you; as you judge, so will you be judged; as you are kind, so will you be treated kindly; it will be measured to you according to the measure you use.' " In 46. 7-8, "Remember the words of Jesus our Lord, for he said, 'Woe to that man! It would be better for him if he had not been born, than that he should cause one of my elect to stumble . . .' "; Ignatius writing to the Smyrneans, 3.2, "And when he came to Peter and his companions he said, 'Take, touch me and see that I am not a disembodied spirit.' "

Mark gives Aramaic words of Jesus in three passages: 5:41, *talitha qum;* 7:34, *effatha;* 14:36, *Abba;* in each case giving the Greek translation.

The spirit of Jesus, as his personal friends knew it, was no doubt a prime factor in forming the developing gospel tradition, this at the very earliest stage as they tried to interpret it to others. Although secondhand, it may be the most authentic factor of all. Its effect may be seen in such a passage as Galatians 5:22, "The fruits of the spirit are love, joy, peace, patience, kindness, goodness, faithfulness, gentleness, and self-control." [1] May not we regard this as a characterization of the personality of Jesus? Or are we willing to entertain the suggestion that in Paul the stream rose higher than its source?

The use of the Septuagint exercised a decided warping influence in certain passages. Early Christians found in their Bible many passages that reminded them of Jesus in his role as Messiah. Some of these passages Jews had long before interpreted as prophecies of the Anointed. Unconsciously perhaps, as such passages were associated with Jesus, the fluid oral tradition was warped to fit the letter of Scripture. Being divinely inspired, it was no doubt felt to be more reliable than oral tradition, and hence was used to correct and amplify it. A splendid example of this is the account of the triumphal entry of Jesus into Jerusalem on the first day of the Passion Week. According to Mark, Jesus rode on a colt. Some early Christian, while reading or

---

[1] *Op. cit.* p. 39.

hearing Zechariah 9:9, decided the correct picture must be that given by the prophet. So according to Matthew, Jesus rode on a donkey and her colt, both at the same time. Moreover, Mark's colt may have been a horse instead of a donkey. This was the contention of Walter Bauer,[1] the leading New Testament lexicographer of his day. Thus even written Gospels were amended to fit Scriptural statements, Matthew being a revised edition of Mark.

Although Matthew exhibits marked poetic tendencies, the author failed to recognize one of the main features of Hebrew poetry, which usually makes a statement and then repeats it in different words, so when the prophet says:

> *Unassuming and riding on a donkey,*
> *And on a colt, the foal of a donkey,*

he is writing about one animal only, and not about a mother and her young. Supposed conformity to the Old Testament changed the number from one to two, and possibly the species from horse to donkey. One of the most absurd examples of how far such warping could go is found in the apocryphal Gospel, Pseudo-Matthew, 18, where dragons come out of a cave as the holy family passes on its way to Egypt, and worship the infant Jesus in fulfilment of Psalm 148:7, "Praise the Lord from the earth, you dragons."

The need early Christians felt for information, guidance, entertainment, etc., no doubt also determined the selection of those items to be reduced to writing. Anti-Jewish polemic was one of the earliest needs. This motive is frequently met in Paul's writings as he argued against the Judaizing party, in Mark's discussion of Sabbath observance and dietary restrictions, in Matthew's Sermon on the Mount, and in many other passages.

Assessment of John the Baptist comes sharply into view in several places. As evidenced in Acts 18:24-19:7, the movement apparently headed by him maintained a separate existence for some time. Each of the canonical Gospels, especially the Fourth, is at some pains to put John in his place, i.e., strictly secondary

---

[1] "The Colt of Palm Sunday (Der Palmesel)," translated by F. W. Gingrich, *Journal of Biblical Literature* 72, Dec. 1953, pp. 220-229.

to Jesus. "He must increase and I must decrease," says the Baptist of the Fourth Gospel, 3:30; but his cult never died in the Old Churches, i.e., the pre-Reformation bodies.

It has been suggested that one reason for inclusion of miracles in the Gospels was to meet the competition furnished by Jewish citation of miracles performed by the prophets. There is also reason to believe that pagan miracle stories presented a similar competition. Pagan heroes and demi-gods, such as Hercules, Romulus, Orpheus, etc., had worked wonders, and Jesus must be shown to be even more powerful. The emperor Vespasian, as he was passing through Egypt, is said by Suetonius Vesp. 8.7.2-3 to have healed a blind man by the application of saliva, and a cripple by treading. Hercules and Romulus were born of virgins, had ascended to heaven, and had been deified.

Jesus as the Christ early became the center of Christian worship. One of the chief aids to this worship was the recounting of features of his career, especially of his death and resurrection. Gospel tradition must have taken form mainly in this phase of worship. Local varieties of tradition developed as regular features of ritual.

Convenient, popular ethical codes were needed. For this purpose the Two Great Commandments were adopted, Leviticus 19:18 and Deuteronomy 6:4-5; and the Ten Commandments from Exodus 20. Need was felt for more detailed instruction in the Christian spirit per se. The two great responses are Romans 12 and Matthew 5-7. The need for such codes is evidenced in detail by the ethical questions treated in First Corinthians.

Doctrinal guidance was even more strongly craved, as shown by Paul's letters, which are "first heavy with doctrine." The theological developments were chiefly to correct Jewish, Gnostic, and Docetic influences. This motif can be traced from Galatians to the end of the patristic period.

Encouragement to martyrs was urgently needed from the very beginning. A good example of the response to this is seen in Mark 8:34, "If anyone wants to follow me, let him deny himself and take up his cross." This is certainly anachronistic. One of the chief functions of the Passion narrative has always been the encouragement of martyrs. Matthew 10:32 is another example. "Whoever confesses me before men, I will acknowledge him before my father in heaven." Others can be found throughout the Gospels. Dire consequences are threatened if anyone weakens.

Entertainment was always in demand, and no doubt was of great help in maintaining and promoting the movement. Christians have always enjoyed the Gospel arguments where Jesus puts his opponents to rout. The same naiveté that accounts for the survival of the Goliath and Samson stories in the Old Testament may also be the reason room was found in the New for the feeding of the multitude, the walking on water, and the calming of the storm. Certainly it accounts for the riot of wonder stories in the apocryphal gospels.

Familiarity with the Psalms led to many direct quotations and more or less obvious allusions. In Matthew's temptation series 4:6 the devil quotes Psalm 91:11-12; in Luke 13:27 Jesus quotes Psalm 6:8; the Passion narrative in each Gospel is obviously influenced by Psalms. Mark and Matthew quote opening words of Psalm 22 as the last word on the cross. Luke quotes Psalm 31:5 as the last word, John uses Psalms 22 and 69 in his crucifixion scene. Two of Matthew's beatitudes, 5:5, 8, may be seen in Psalm 37:11, "The meek will inherit the land;" and Psalm 24:4, "The pure in heart," who "will stand in his holy place." Among less obvious reminiscences of the Psalter are Matthew 10:29 and Luke 12:6, where God's knowledge of the sparrows parallels Psalm 50:11, "I know all the birds." Luke 2:35, "A sword will go through your own soul," parallels the Septuagint version of Psalm 105:18, "Iron went through his soul." These are only a few of many examples.

Mechanical convenience in the size of a scroll book was likely a factor in gospel writing. A papyrus roll of more than twenty-five feet in length is unwieldy. If a book had to be much longer it was divided into two.

The developing traditions show a number of tendencies such as progressive exaltation of Jesus, leading to final deification; identification of individuals who are anonymous in earlier accounts; revision of language toward Attic standards; increasing anti-Semitism; removal of offensive items; and enhancing of

67

miracles. An example of the last tendency is seen in the case of Jairus' daughter. In Mark 5:23 she is near death, in Luke 8:42 dying, in Matthew 9:18 already dead when her father comes to Jesus for help.

In considering the development of miracle tradition it must always be remembered the ancient public was quite ready to believe reports of miracles. Note the ease with which the Lycaonians in Acts 14:11-18 assumed Paul and Barnabas to be Hermes and Zeus.

Interwoven with the above features is an all-pervading anachronism reflecting the views and attitudes of the time of writing rather than those of the days of Jesus. This is most obvious in the Fourth Gospel, where Jews are usually spoken of as a people apart. While the first three Gospels mention "the Jews" five or six times apiece, John uses the term 69 times! The Fourth Gospel also speaks three times of "the Passover of the Jews," all of these in passages about the Passion Week or earlier. Now in English there is no Passover except that of the Jews, but in Greek there are two. The Greek word is *Pascha*, which is used both for Passover and Easter. And this is the striking anachronism. There was no Christian Pascha before the second century, and so no need until then to specify the Jewish Pascha. The writer of the Fourth Gospel is looking back from a second century standpoint.

The most disappointing conclusion of historical research in the New Testament field is that none of the Gospels is the work of a companion of Jesus. What eyewitness testimony is embodied in these works cannot be identified and separated from the rest.

In attempting to understand the origins of the Gospels it is important to remember that the stories about Jesus circulated orally and as separate units for thirty or forty years before our earliest Gospel was written.

Almost anyone can think of some relative, prominent in the family connexion, about whom various anecdotes are preserved, some great-grandparent, uncle, or aunt, who has been a source of amusement or pride, and about whose memory a legend has developed. If one takes the trouble to list the anecdotes he can recall, he will see how self-contained each one is, and how lacking in exact dates. Some incidents may be connected with well-known events, such as a war, a presidential election, a wedding, a journey; but the exact month, day, and year are not part of the oral tradition as such. There may be several anecdotes to illustrate a single trait, some furnish background for the subject's sayings, some are stories the person himself told. Of such items the first written gospels were made. We do not know who first wrote down a collection of stories about Jesus.

2. MARK

Mark is the main source of canonical gospel material. Matthew uses almost all of Mark, Luke a large proportion, and John a number of passages. The contents of our earliest Gospel are as follows:

1. 1-8   John the Baptist
    9-11   Baptism of Jesus
    12-13   Temptation of Jesus
    14-20   Call of Simon, Andrew, James, and John
    21-28   Curing and Exorcizing in Capernaum Synagogue on Sabbath
    29-31   Curing Simon's Mother-in-law
    32-34   Various Cures and Exorcisms
    35-39   Tour of Nearby Villages
    40-45   Curing a Leper
2. 1-12   Curing a Paralytic Carried by Four
    13-14   Call of Levi
    15-17   Eating with Irreligious
    18-22   Fasting
    23-28   Picking Grain on Sabbath
3. 1-6   Curing in Synagogue on Sabbath
    7-12   Curing by the Lake
    13-19   Appointing the Twelve Apostles
    20-30   Jesus Accused of Working with Beelzebub
    31-35   Visit of Immediate Family
4. 1-34   Parables by the Lake
    35-41   Calming a Storm
5. 1-20   Exorcism of Legion from a Gadarene
    21-43   Curing Jairus' Daughter and a Woman with Hemorrhage

6.	1-6	Visit to Nazareth Synagogue
	7-13	Mission of the Twelve
	14-29	Murder of John the Baptist
	30-44	Feeding Five Thousand
	45-52	Walking on the Lake and Calming the Storm
	53-56	Cures at Gennesaret
7.	1-23	Washing Hands before Eating
	24-30	Syro-Phoenician Exorcism
	31-37	Cure with Saliva
8.	1-9	Feeding Four Thousand
	10	Crossing to Dalmanoutha
	11-13	Encounter with Pharisees
	14-21	Pharisaic Leaven
	22-26	Cure with Saliva
	27-30	"Who do People Say I Am?"
	31-33	Prophecy of Passion
	34-38	Whoever Would Follow Me
9.	1	Coming again while Auditors still Living
	2-13	Transfiguration
	14-29	An Exorcism
	30-32	Prophecy of Passion
	33-37	Who is Greatest?
	38-50	Discourse Section on Several Subjects
10.	1-12	On Divorce
	13-16	Let the Children Come to Me
	17-22	Counsel of Poverty
	23-27	Qualification of Counsel on Poverty
	28-31	Rewards for those who Renounce
	32-34	Prophecy of Passion
	35-45	James and John Want to Sit beside Him in Glory
	46-52	Cure of Blind Bartimaeus
11.	1-11	The Triumphal Entry
	12-14	Curse on the Barren Fig Tree
	15-19	Expulsion of Dealers from Temple
	20-25	Lesson of the Fig Tree
	27-33	High Priests, Scholars, and Elders Question Jesus' Authority
12.	1-12	Parable of the Vineyard
	13-17	Shall we Pay the Roman Tax?
	18-27	No Marriage in Heaven
	28-34	The Most Important Commandment

    35-37   Relationship of David and the Anointed
    38-40   Warning against the Scholars
    41-44   The Widow's Two Lepta (Cents)
13. 1-37   The Eschatological Discourse
14. 1-2   High Priests and Scholars Fear to Kill Jesus at
            Passover
     3-9   A Woman Anoints Him in Bethany
     10-11 Judas' Bargain with the High Priests
     12-16 Preparation for Passover Supper
     17-26 The Passover Supper, Thursday
     27-31 Peter's Boast
     32-42 Gethsemane
     43-52 Seizure by Jewish Authorities
     53-65 Hearing before the High Priest
     66-72 Peter's Denial
15. 1-15   Trial before Pilate
     16-20 Mockery by Soldiers
     21-41 The Crucifixion, Friday
     42-47 Burial by Joseph of Arimathea
16. 1-8   The Women Find the Tomb Empty, Sunday

In the two opening paragraphs Mark indicates lines of teaching to be followed throughout the Gospel, namely, that Jesus is the promised Messiah, the son of God, a person of great power, under the control of the Spirit, and victorious in the continuous war against the supernatural powers of evil. His characteristic word, "immediately," which he always uses in the shorter form, also appears at the outset. He uses the word as often as it is used in all the rest of the New Testament. It is symptomatic of his characteristically abrupt transitions, abrupt beginning, and abrupt ending.

The arrangement is partly chronological, partly topical, partly geographical. After the three introductory paragraphs the Gospel may be divided geographically into three parts: (1) the Galilean ministry, 1:14-9:50, (2) the journey to Jerusalem, 10:1-52, (3) the week at Jerusalem, 11:1-16:8. But already in the latter part of the Galilean ministry, after Jesus asked who people thought he was, attention is directed toward the Passion.

Mark repeats and illustrates time and again the lines of

thought initiated in his opening paragraphs, viz., the nature of the Anointed, his power, his possession by the Spirit, and his victorious war with the supernatural powers of evil.

Peter says, 8:30, "You are the Anointed." Blind Bartimaeus cries, 10:47, "Son of David, Jesus, have mercy on me." At the Triumphal Entry the crowd shouts, 11:9-10, "Blessed is the one coming in the name of the Lord." "Blessed is the coming kingdom of our father David." Jesus teaching in the Temple says, 12:35, "How can the scholars say the Anointed is David's son? David himself, speaking by the Holy Spirit, says, 12:36-37, 'The Lord said to my lord, "Sit at my right"' . . . David himself calls him 'lord,' so how can he be his son?" At his appearance before the sanhedrin the high priest asks him, 14:61, "Are you the Anointed, the son of the Blessed One?" Jesus answers, 14:62, "I am, and you will see the son of man sitting at the right of the Almighty and coming in the clouds of the sky." Pilate asked him, 15:2, "Are you the king of the Jews?" Jesus answered, "You have said it." And King of the Jews is the title placed on the cross, 15:26. Finally, the centurion who watched him die said, 15:39, "This man really was God's son."

He is "declared to be the son of God with power," power over men, as shown by the suddenness with which the first disciples left their fathers and occupations and followed him, and by his refutation of other religious leaders; his power over nature as shown by the withering of the barren fig tree after he cursed it, by walking on water, and multiplying bread and fish to feed thousands; his power over disease by numerous cures; power over the Sabbath and power to forgive sins. Even his death was powerful, for he expired with a loud shout.

From the time of his baptism he is under the control of the Holy Spirit, which drives him into the desert to be tempted, 1:12. When scholars from Jerusalem made the charge, 3:22, that he was possessed by Beelzebub, and so empowered to perform exorcisms, he explained that the prince of evil would not expel his own subjects, and that anyone who said the power of an exorcist was from Satan, had committed the unpardonable sin of blaspheming the Holy Spirit. This is no doubt an answer to those who maligned exorcism in the early Church.

His victorious war against the supernatural powers of evil began immediately after his baptism as the Spirit drove him into the desert to be tempted by Satan. Jesus' first miracle in Mark is an exorcism performed while teaching on Sabbath at a synagogue in Capernaum. The foul spirit recognized him and cried out, 1:24, "What do we have to do with you, Jesus of Nazareth? I know you, who you are, God's holy one." The stilling of the storms on the lake probably belongs in this context, for it seems to show his power over one of the capricious demons that were believed to control bodies of water. The most spectacular of Mark's exorcisms is the expelling of a legion of foul spirits from one man. When the demons, 5:10-12, requested permission to enter a drove of about two thousand hogs, it was granted and the herd rushed over the cliff into the lake and was drowned. The empty tomb is Mark's final proof of Jesus Christ's ability to vanquish supernatural powers of evil.

Mark wanted to show that Jesus was distinctly superior to other men, worthy in the fullest sense of his Davidic ancestry, and in some special sense the son of God. Yet he specifically denies that Jesus is equal to God. "Why do you call me good? Only one is good, and that is God," 10:18; the places of honor were not his to give, 10:35-41; "Abba, Father, all things are possible for you. Take this cup away from me. But do your will, not mine," 14:36.

Two sections of Mark, 6:31-7:37 and 8:1-26, seem to be variants of the same series of items. Each has a miraculous feeding of a multitude, a trip on the lake, a controversy with Pharisees, and a cure with saliva. In the first series five thousand are fed, the fragments are gathered up in "baskets," the controversy is on washing hands before eating, and a deaf and dumb man is cured. In the list of vices, 7:22, given in the controversy, the evil eye is included, a superstition still alive in the Near East in the twentieth century. In the second series four thousand are fed, the fragments are gathered in "hampers," the controversy is on signs, and a blind man is cured with saliva.

Matthew uses both series, but omits the healings with saliva, 14:13-15:30. Matthew 14:28-32 adds Peter's venture at walking on water. Luke uses only the first item of the first series, the feeding of the five thousand, 9:10-17. John uses the first two items of the first series, 6:1-21, the latter including Jesus' walking on the lake. John adds that when the disciples were part way across the lake, Jesus met them. When he got in, the boat was instantly transported the rest of the way. In John various controversies follow the crossing. The Fourth Gospel treats sources with freedom, somewhat as Josephus handles Old Testament narratives. In this passage John preserves the key word *kóphini* (baskets), thus indicating derivation from Mark.

Both Luke and John seem to consider the feeding of the four thousand, with fragments in "hampers," too much like the feeding of the five thousand to warrant inclusion.

In the liturgical core passage, Mark 6:41, "After taking the five loaves and the two fish, he looked up at the sky and blessed and broke the loaves and gave them to the disciples to set before them," Luke, as so often, preserves Mark's wording more closely than Matthew.

Presumably the story of the feeding of a multitude was first told in Aramaic, with perhaps the same word always used for basket. Two different raconteurs telling the story in Greek used two different words for basket, as for example, basket and hamper. English translators, except Weymouth, have obliterated this difference, but translators into some other languages have been more faithful. The Peshitto simply borrowed the two Greek words. Somewhere back of Mark there must be two written accounts, one having five thousand men and twelve "baskets," the other four thousand men and seven "hampers."

The "hamper" version seems less finished, using the sacred number seven for both loaves and "hampers," and adding the few fish somewhat as an afterthought. In the "basket" account the five loaves and two fish make seven, while there is a basket for each of the apostles, avoiding repetition of the number seven. The number of people is also better rounded. Luke and John chose this superior form for their Gospels.

The above view seems to gain added weight, as well as an additional problem, with the repetition of the "basket" and "hamper" distinction in the comment of Mark 8:19-20 and Matthew 16:9-10. This comment must be part of the editorial treatment of the warning against the leaven of the Pharisees. Compare Luke 12:1.

Mark's accounts of cures with saliva must have been offensive to some, for Matthew omits them, though such treatment was popular enough at the time Mark was written. Perhaps Mark wanted to show that Jesus was at least as powerful as the emperor Vespasian. John has a healing with saliva and dust made into mud.

Next, as the reader's attention is turned toward the Passion, comes the question by Jesus, 8:27, "Who do people say I am?" Peter answers, "You are the Anointed." Here for the first time clearly emerges the puzzle of the Messianic secret, as Jesus charges his disciples to tell no one. Here also begin the prophecies of the Passion.

In the Synoptics Jesus does not want his disciples to tell that he is the Messiah. There is nothing about this in John.

Mark 11:25 contains what may be a nucleus of the Our Father.

In the anointing in the house of Simon the leper, 14:3-9, a woman pours the perfume on Jesus' head. The same is true in Matthew 26:7, but in Luke 7:38 and John 12:3 his feet are anointed. The first form of the story envisages an oriental supper, with the guests sitting on the floor around a low table, the other form a Graeco-Roman scene with guests reclining on benches about the table.

The earliest of our Gospels is naturally the least cultured. Its Greek is more colloquial in diction, grammar, and sentence structure; its beginning is abrupt and its transitions rough. Whether the ending was always as abrupt as in the present critical text is a question. From early times this ending has been felt abrupt, so much so that at least three early attempts were made to smooth it off.

Although colloquial, this Gospel is written in sound Greek idiom.[1]

The language has a vividness that is hardly compensated for by Matthew's pedantic revisions. For example, "the skies were being opened," instead of Mark's "the skies were split." Mark is often colorful, but Matthew destroys some of the color by his condensations, or however the briefer form is explained. In

---

[1] For extensive illustration see James A. Kleist, *The Gospel of Saint Mark*, Part Two (Milwaukee, 1936).

the "basket" passage Matthew omits the clause, "The people were like sheep without a shepherd," and Mark's vigorous rhetorical question, "Shall we go and buy two hundred loaves of bread for them to eat?" Matthew also omits Mark's picturesque colloquialism that Jesus directed that the crowd be seated "picnic groups by picnic groups." Mark's "green grass" becomes simply "grass" in Matthew, and the final touch in describing the gala scene, viz., "They reclined in groups like one flower bed after another," the prim Matthew omits altogether. In all this it must be admitted that a final editor may have added these touches to an earlier edition of Mark.

Mark presented some embarrassing features to later writers. Perhaps the original ending was excised because it encouraged Docetism or some other heresy. The statement that the women, after they left the empty tomb, "said nothing to anyone," is in flat contradiction to the other Gospels, where they immediately tell the other disciples.

In 2:26 Mark says Abiathar was high priest when David ate the bread of offering, but in First Samuel 21:1 the priest's name is Ahimelech. Matthew and Luke correct by omitting the name of the priest. They employ the same method of correction when quoting Malachi 3:1, which Mark 1:2 ascribes to Isaiah.

In the passage on the two great commandments, Mark 12:29 gives the Shema, the short Jewish creed, "Listen Israel, the Lord our God is one Lord." Matthew and Luke omit it. This bit of Scripture from Deuteronomy 6:4 had no doubt begun to be offensive to Christians because Jews were using it as a testimony against the deification of Jesus. It must have been for the same reason that they also omitted Mark 12:32, "There is no other except him." The scholar's emphatic commendation of Jesus' answer in the same verse seems to detract from the dignity and superiority of Jesus, so Matthew and Luke left it out.

These and other improvements contributed to the oblivion into which our earliest Gospel soon sank, in contrast to the continued popularity of the other three.

Our earliest statement as to the authorship of this Gospel is by Papias, an early second century Apostolic Father whose works have been lost except for brief quotations by other writers. Eusebius, in his Church History 3.39.15, quotes Papias on the origin of the Gospel of Mark. He says that Mark was Peter's interpreter, and that he compiled his Gospel from things he had heard Peter tell. No doubt Peter had picked up some Greek, but in public speaking was limited to Aramaic. How much to discount this statement by Papias is an unsolved problem. Certainly he was mistaken in his judgment of the literary quality of the Gospel, and probably in his belief that the author had no written sources. Although the book is lacking in polish, a thoughtful plan was carefully carried out. The strongest argument in favor of the traditional authorship is the seeming unlikelihood of falsely ascribing the oldest Gospel to one who had not been a companion of Jesus. There were several more impressive names to choose from.

Mark seems to have been composed after the year 70. There are two chief reasons for this view. First, there are indications it was written after the martyrdom of Peter and Paul. Irenaeus, who dated the Gospels as early as he could, says in Against Heresies 3.1.1 that it was "after their departure," and the statement of Papias implies it was after Peter's death. It is generally assumed that Peter and Paul suffered under Nero in the middle sixties.

The second consideration is the destruction of Jerusalem, which may have been a greater shock to the early Christians than the deaths of Peter and Paul. It was in the year 70 after a four year siege that a Roman army under Titus took the city and burned the Temple. This destruction seems to be reflected in Mark. Not that the description is more circumstantial than could have been composed beforehand, but because it is discussed at such length. Here was terrible and unmistakable fulfillment of a prophecy by Jesus, thus proving his ability to foresee events; so Mark gives it more space than any other of Jesus' discourses.

All the Synoptic Gospels must have been written while there were still people living who had seen Jesus in the flesh, for they all say he promised to return in glory while some of his hearers were still alive. As soon as it was obvious that no one was still living who had heard Jesus, Christian writers quit saying he had promised such an early return. Enough had already been said to embarrass traditional exegetes for all time.

The presence of miracle stories in the Gospels is also an indication of their date. It may be taken as a canon of historical judgment that miracles are not reported by eyewitnesses. Examination of such narratives in a setting where one can be impartial, such as a Christian studying Buddhism, or vice-versa, shows that writings containing miracle stories are late and secondary. This is not to entirely reject faith healing, in which so many have believed. Jesus must have been a faith healer. That is one thing. Iron floating on water and a man walking on water belong in another category. Such stories are not reported by eyewitnesses. Paul believed in miracles, but reported none except his own visions, and he was not sure of their objectivity.

The dating of Mark is also conditioned by the fact that it was written before Matthew and Luke, for they both use Mark. Matthew is in fact a revised edition of Mark.

As explained in connexion with prophecies of the second coming, it seems certain the Synoptics were all written before the turn of the century.

3. MATTHEW

To one who carefully compares the Gospels, especially if he has access to the Greek, it becomes evident that the main source of Matthew is Mark. The most convenient way to observe this evidence is with a harmony that arranges the Gospels in parallel columns.

In what ways did the compiler of Matthew revise Mark? The most obvious feature of the revision is the addition of the two-chapter section of infancy narratives at the beginning; next is the insertion of collected discourse materials in six sections, viz., chapters 5-7, 10, 13, 18, 23, and 24-25; and finally the addition of postresurrection appearances of Jesus.

These features may be outlined as follows:

1-2	Infancy narratives	
5-7	Sermon on the Mount	Mk 11:25
10	Mission of the Twelve	Mk 3:16-19, 6:7-11, 13:11-13
13	Parables by the Lake	Mk 4:1-34
18	About the Kingdom	Mk 9:33-50, 10:42-44
23	Against Scholars & Pharisees	Mk 12:38-40
24-25	The Last Things	Mk 13
28	Postresurrection Appearances	

The fact that the best text of Mark has no postresurrection appearances has been unknown to the general public, because popular editions of the Bible are based on late manuscripts containing one of the apocryphal endings of Mark that has postresurrection appearances. The improved text promises, 16:7, but does not give such an appearance.

There are many details not shown in the above simplified outline. One set of details concerns the Marcan items omitted by Matthew.

Each of the six discourse sections has a Marcan nucleus, but the infancy narratives are entirely foreign to Mark, except the reference to Jesus' Davidic ancestry, 12:35-37.

The deliberateness with which five of the discourse sections, omitting chapter 23, were planned is shown by the formulas with which these sections open and close. The opening formula, not always in the same words, states that the disciples approached Jesus and that he spoke to them. The closing formula states that Jesus finished the discourse and left the scene. At the end of the discourse on the last things, instead of saying that he left, it is said that he announced his departure from this life. Chapter 23, though also a definite discourse section, does not open and close with these formulas.

The non-Marcan material falls into two classes, what Matthew shares with Luke, and what is found only in Matthew. The non-Marcan material common to Matthew and Luke is usually designated by the symbol Q, standing for the German word *Quelle*, "source," referring to the indication that Matthew and Luke must have had another common source beside Mark. Examples of Q are the Beatitudes, the Our Father, and the triple temptation of Jesus. The three examples of Q just given are found in Matthew 5, Luke 6; Matthew 6, Luke 11; and Matthew 4, Luke 4.

If one examines the structure of Matthew in greater detail he finds that some passages of Mark have been copied twice, in different connexions. This is no doubt due to the rearrangement of discourse material. There are a number of additions besides the infancy narratives that are peculiar to Matthew, e.g., 17:27, the coin in the fish's mouth; 14:29, Peter trying to walk on water; 27:5, Judas' suicide; 27:19, Pilate's wife's dream. A few passages of Mark are missing in Matthew, e.g., two accounts of healing with saliva, 7:33-35 and 8:23.

In Mark and Matthew the risen Lord appears, or is to appear, to the disciples in Galilee, while in Luke and John he first appears to them in Jerusalem.

SPECIAL FEATURES

The book opens with an exhibition of the art of genealogy, a section almost totally devoid of interest for most readers, but offering a rich series of contacts with the Old Testament. Next come the joys and tragedy of the infancy narratives, then the expanded temptation scenes and a few items of the early Galilean ministry. These furnish the setting for the Sermon on the Mount, whose three chapters, from their vantage point in the opening pages of the New Testament, dominate the whole field of Christian ideals. Matthew's beatitudes are the ones learned by heart, his Our Father is the one universally used.

Matthew's love of form and symmetry led him to divide the names of his genealogy into three sections of fourteen names each, although he had to omit five names from the second section to keep it down to fourteen. His genius for symmetrical statement virtually produces poetry in the parallelisms of the beatitudes and stanza-like structure of the six paragraphs on spiritual fulfillment of the Law, 5:21-47, and in the following six on charity, prayer, and fasting. Balanced structure and parallelism run through all the first discourse section, rising to classic height in the Our Father. The same tendency is seen in the discourse section, 23:14-39, the seven woes pronounced on scholars and Pharisees, with the concluding lament over Jerusalem. Note in 21:41 how he replaced Mark's 12:9,

> *eleúsetai kai apolései tous georgoús*
> *He will come and destroy the tenants,*

with the unforgettable little chiasmus, and its collocation of kappas so popular among ancient Greeks,[2]

---

[2] Cf. Lohmeyer-Schmauch, Mattäus-Evangelium, p. 315, etc.

kakoús kakós apolései autoús
he will miserably destroy those wicked men.

The appeal of acoustic effect and orderly arrangement are no doubt factors in the overwhelming success of this revised Gospel.

In the Old Testament quotations the reviser's formalism is united with a special interest in prophecy. Time and again he reminds the reader that such and such happened "to fulfill what was spoken through the prophet." Sometimes these citations are far fetched, as when the historical statement of Hosea 11:1, about the Exodus, is taken as a prophecy of the return of the holy family from Egypt. When he revised Mark's account of the triumphal entry his zeal for prophecy led him astray. Not realizing the parallelism of almost all ancient Hebrew poetry, he misunderstood Zechariah 9:9, thinking the prophet was talking about two animals when he wrote,

> *Humble and riding on a donkey,*
> *And on a colt, the foal of a donkey.*

So Matthew says, 21:7, that the disciples brought the donkey and her colt and put their garments on them, and that Jesus sat on them. None of the other evangelists were so misled: Mark 11:1-7, Luke 19:29-35, John 12:12-14. It seems strange that one with the poetic interests of this reviser should, in spite of great familiarity with the Old Testament, be unaware of this characteristic feature of ancient Hebrew poetry; but it has been a common failing of Bible students throughout the centuries. Standard English translations have blurred this mistake of Matthew by translating "sat thereon," instead of "sat on them."

The Fourth Gospel, in quoting the prophecy of Zechariah, leaves out the second line of the parallelism, quoting only "Behold your king is coming, sitting on a donkey's colt." Yet the Fourth Gospel crucifixion scene, 19:24, betrays the same obliviousness to parallelism, for in quoting Psalm 22:18,

> *They divided my clothing among themselves*
> *And on my apparel they cast lots,*

the author thinks it necessary to envisage two separate processes instead of the one certainly intended by the psalmist. The Synoptic Gospels give a different wording of the Psalm, which destroys the parallelism and so allows them to picture a single process of division. In any case the Gospel scene corresponds to the evangelist's understanding of the Scripture quoted. Both Matthew's Triumphal Entry and John's Crucifixion are splendid examples of gospel tradition being warped to fit understanding of the Old Testament.

In revising Mark's language Matthew often substitutes other and more literary words for Mark's colloquialisms, irons out harsh constructions, substitutes subordinate structure for coordinate, and seems to choose certain renderings for their acoustic effect.

Matthew's genius furnishes us with a number of the most quotable and most quoted passages in all literature, his first and third discourse sections being the richest, but by no means the only sources. Outstanding unique passages are the visit of the magi, the flight to Egypt, the slaughter of the innocents, and the great commission.

He seems to have a special interest in the primacy of Peter, 16:13-20 being the best-known New Testament passage on the subject. Another is the prominence given Peter by his attempt to walk on water, 14:28-31. Anti-Jewish polemic is a leading motive throughout.

Some Gospel readers have puzzled over the difference between the kingdom of heaven and the kingdom of God. The fact is that Matthew uses the pietistic Jewish phrase "kingdom of heaven," while other New Testament writers use "kingdom of God."

A glaring blemish of this Gospel is its caricature of the Pharisees. Condemning all Pharisees for the faults of a few is a feature of all four Gospels; but no such picture is drawn of them in the rest of the New Testament, where they are mentioned only in Acts and Philippians. In the Gospel presentations we see a bitter phase of anti-Jewish polemic as carried on by Christians toward the end of the first century. In Acts Pharisees are pictured as the best and most pious of Jews. From Jewish history it appears Acts is nearer the truth.

All four Gospels tell of certain women seeing the empty tomb on the first Easter morning. Mark promises and Matthew gives a Galilean appearance of the risen Jesus to the disciples. This is in contrast to Luke and John, who give Jerusalem appearances. John however, in the Appendix, chapter 21, does add a Galilean appearance.

DATE AND PLACE OF COMPOSITION

It has been suggested that Matthew was composed at Antioch, and that the peculiar material was drawn from the Antiochene tradition. One of the main reasons for this suggestion is the apparent use of this Gospel by Ignatius of Antioch, who is the first writer seeming to have any acquaintance with Matthew. If Ignatius wrote somewhere near 110, we may infer Matthew was written before 100. We may say it was written after Mark and before the letters of Ignatius. Of course it is possible Matthew and Ignatius were giving the same Syrian traditions independently. Ignatius does not mention the Gospel by name. Papias is the first to do that, possibly a generation later. It may well be that, at the time Ignatius wrote, the Gospel did not yet have a name.

The polemic against Docetism seems to start with Luke, John, and Ignatius, thus indicating Matthew may be earlier than Luke. However, the fact that Matthew and Luke show no acquaintance with each other is strong indication they were written about the same time.

As stated before, the Synoptics must all have been written while some who heard Jesus were still living. John and other later books do not promise such an early second coming. This would date all the Synoptics before the end of the century.

It is noteworthy that the Christology of Ignatius is more advanced than that of Matthew, but this is not evidence of later date. The Christology of Paul's letters is more advanced than that of the Synoptics. Ignatius' Christology is Pauline. He uses Paul's letters more than he does the Gospel of Matthew.

Certainly the book as we know it was not written by anyone who had associated with Jesus. Such an author would not have had to depend on second- and thirdhand information furnished by such an author as Mark, who was not one of the close friends. The earliest attempt to solve the problem of authorship is found in one of the surviving fragments of Papias, the earliest known writer on such questions. Eusebius, Church History 3.39.16, preserves the Papias passage as follows: "So then, Matthew composed his oracles in the Hebrew dialect, and each one translated them as he was able." That is the best evidence we have of Matthean authorship, but it can hardly apply to our present Gospel, which is a revised edition of a Greek work. It is possible to imagine the reviser made some use of Aramaic sayings of Jesus, but that would not be Matthean authorship of the present Gospel. It is all part of strained attempts to show apostolic authorship, or at least apostolic background, for certain books in a day when flourishing heresies led the orthodox to discredit whatever could not muster some show of apostolicity. In Stromateis 7.17 Clement of Alexandria says the teaching of the apostles ended under Nero. This emperor died in 68.

Regardless of authorship, Christendom will continue to use Matthew's version of the Our Father and of the Beatitudes, as well as many other passages in this, the most popular of the Synoptics. Renan called it the greatest book ever written.[3]

4. LUKE-ACTS

Luke also is based on Mark. In general he follows the Marcan order, but frequently fills it in with material from other sources. His most extensive departure from Mark is the central portion, 9:51-18:14. This section has a great deal of non-Marcan material, and contains many of the passages that give Luke its distinctive coloring.

Most notable among the unique passages of the central por-

---

[3] "Le plus important qui ait jamais été écrit." Les Evangiles, p. 213.

tion are the parables of the good Samaritan, the prodigal son, the rich man and Lazarus, the rich fool, and those who "all with one consent began to make excuse."

Other less famous passages peculiar to this section are the mission of the seventy, Mary choosing the better part, the man called out of bed at night, the rebuke to incipient Mariolatry, those who are beaten with few stripes, those on whom the wall fell, the choice of seats at a feast, the lost coin, the unrighteous wise steward, the slave that plows all day and then gets his master's supper before his own, the ten lepers, "The kingdom of God is within you," the Pharisee and the revenue officer praying.

Finally, there are in the central portion a few strangely distinctive minor passages with a flavor all their own, such as, "Give alms for what is within," "tombs unwittingly walked over," "Fear not little flock," "purses that don't get old," "I came to start a fire, and how I wish it were started already!" "Why not make up your own minds about what is right?" "Go and say to that fox," "Make friends with your tainted money."

By one count forty-three items of the central portion are peculiar to Luke, forty-three common to Matthew, one paralleled in John, and eleven found in all three Synoptics. All Marcan parallels are also in Matthew. The framework in which the various items are set is apparently editorial, as are some of the comments and morals drawn. See Appendix V for an outline of the central portion.

To the Marcan outline Luke prefaced a series of infancy narratives. This is the most familiar feature of Luke. They are entirely different from the infancy stories in Matthew, except for the virginity of Mary, the birth at Bethlehem, and the residence in Nazareth. Almost any list of Christmas carols makes clear which Gospel has had the greatest influence in this field. In Matthew there is no inn, no manger, no company of shepherds, no chorus of angels. Luke also has the canticles: Magnificat, Benedictus, and Nunc Dimittis, as well as the first part of the most used Christian prayer, the Ave Maria. In this connexion should be remembered lines from the Stabat Mater, "Cuius animam gementem, Contristatem, et dolentem, Pertransivit gladius." (Through whose anguished, afflicted, and grieving soul the sword passed.) Compare Luke 2:35 and Psalm 22:20. Luke's influence on hymn writers has been out of all proportion to that of the other Gospels. Infancy narratives are of course entirely foreign to Mark and John.

The amount of space devoted to John the Baptist may be partly explained by the part he played in the beginning of Jesus' public life, partly by the strength of the Baptist movement as a rival to Christianity, but partly also by Luke's interest in history.

It seems fair to say Luke is the most beautiful of the Gospels. This impression is largely due to the first two chapters, but is strengthened throughout the Gospel, one of the most beautiful passages being the walk to Emmaus in the last chapter.

Luke has the most literary Greek of all the Gospels. His language is less literary when using common Synoptic material, but even here he makes many changes away from colloquialism. When composing freely, as in the preface to the first volume, the language is quite above the level of the rest of the book. Of course this phenomenon is often seen in other writers. Among New Testament writings, it is only in Hebrews that one finds so near an approach to a classical period. Luke makes fewer changes in the meaning of Marcan material than does Matthew, probably also fewer in Q.

Various conjectures are made as to why Luke omitted certain passages found in Mark. In some instances he substitutes other accounts, as both he and Matthew do for the temptation of Jesus. Some items in Mark may have become offensive in Luke's milieu, as perhaps healing with the use of saliva and certain features of the passion narratives. Lack of room in the volume he planned may well have been a consideration. Some lines in Mark may have seemed irrelevant, as for example the introduction to the Shema, Mark 12:29; or even unreasonable, e.g., the cursing of the barren fig tree. He saw fit to choose the tradition that the risen Lord's first appearance to any of the apostles was at Jerusalem, no doubt the reason for his omission of Mark 14:28. His views of historical probability were no doubt sometimes a factor in his choices.

Luke differs from the other Synoptics in a number of ways. The differences are mainly in the direction of John. This is especially clear in the resurrection narratives. All four Gospels tell of certain women finding the tomb empty, but only Luke and John give the first appearance of the risen Jesus in Jerusalem. In Luke and John a woman anoints Jesus' feet, in Mark and Matthew his head. Luke and John share some anti-Docetic features, though Luke has a most Docetic account in the Emmaus incident and John in the risen Lord entering the room though the door is locked. Luke's picture of the risen Lord eating fish, and the last chapter of John showing him cooking fish, are further items.

Docetism held that Jesus only seemed to have a human nature and to share in its physical vicissitudes. John's story of the soldier piercing Jesus' body with a spear is probably given to show he had blood. Docetists no doubt remembered Paul had written, "Flesh and blood cannot inherit the kingdom of God," First Corinthians 15:50.

Ascension narratives are peculiar to Luke-Acts, one at the end of the Gospel and the other at the beginning of Acts. Other ascension narratives in ancient literature are Josephus' account of the disappearance of Moses, the ascension of Elijah in Second Kings, Livy's story of the disappearance of Romulus, and Greek legends of the ascension of Hercules. These narratives are given in Appendix IV.

The dangers of wealth are emphasized more in Luke than in the other Gospels. Two of his contributions to Gospel material on this subject are the parable of the rich fool and the parable of the rich man and Lazarus. Note that Luke in his version of the Beatitudes says, "Blessed are the poor." Matthew's form of this beatitude could, if taken literally, apply to any miser. New Testament views on wealth may have been influenced by Jewish monasticism. It is Luke who reports the repudiation of private property by early Christians in Jerusalem, Acts 4:32 ff. This interest may be a factor in the prominence Luke gives the Baptist.

A better known feature of Luke is the prominence given women. He alone has the Annunciation, Mary's visit to Elizabeth, the saintly Anna, the raising of the widow's son, Mary choosing the better part, the woman healed on Sabbath, and the one who lost the coin.

The authorship of the Gospel should be considered in connexion with that of its companion volume, Acts. It is evident from their openings, with the dedications to Theophilos, that they are two volumes of the same work.

It has been generally accepted that the Luke mentioned by Paul as the "beloved physician," who was with him when he wrote Colossians and Philemon, is the author of Luke-Acts. However, the traditional view has been strongly criticized by some of the ablest scholars. The most convincing argument for Lucan authorship is, as in the case of Mark, the improbability of his name being used as a pseudonym. Would not the name of an apostle have been chosen instead, as in the case of Matthew? The we sections, taken in connexion with Paul's mention of Luke with him at Rome, Colossians 4:14, Philemon 1:24, seem to confirm the traditional view. However, this notice may be the basis of an ancient conjecture made in the attempt to find an apostolic connexion for the book.

It has been suggested that Luke, as a gentile convert, would not have had so much familiarity with Scripture. It is inferred from Colossians 4:10-14 that Luke was a gentile convert. A studious gentile could have made himself at home in the Septuagint, as we know others did.

A more arresting argument against the Lucan authorship is the incongruity between Paul's attitude on circumcision and diet as seen in his letters and as reported in Acts. The latter seems unaware of the sharpness of the Judaistic controversy witnessed in Galatians. How could Luke have been ignorant of Paul's attitude? How explain the contrast in Christology between Luke and Paul? It may be that Luke did not accept all of Paul's views. He probably never saw a collection of Paul's letters. It has been suggested that the publication of Acts led to their collection. The failure to reflect Paul's Christology may be due to his care for his sources.

DATE

As stated before, the latest date for any of the Synoptics is, in all probability, while persons were still living who had heard Jesus. The earliest date for Luke is the publication of Mark. It is reasonable to suppose that either Matthew or Luke would have made use of the other's book had it been known to him. Their varying Judas stories and Luke's two cups at the last supper are among the striking differences, but the most obvious divergence is the completely different series of infancy stories. So it seems Luke and Matthew must have been written about the same time.

Most readers, having the haziest notions of geography, fail to note the discrepancy in the location of the postresurrection appearances to the disciples, Mark and Matthew agreeing against Luke and John.

The puzzling question of the silence of Acts about Paul's death should be mentioned here. In the first place, the beginning of his life is also ignored, except to say he was from Tarsus and was born a Roman citizen. The most convincing answer to this question is that Paul is not the subject of Acts. Had he been, the failure to tell of his death would indicate he was still living when the book was finished. The subject of Acts is, in the words of James Moffatt,[4] "How the Church grew and spread." The establishment in Rome may then be regarded as a fitting climax.

Perhaps the possibility should be considered that Paul's death was inglorious. Could that account for Clement's vagueness? As a matter of fact, we do not know when or where or how he died; yet it seems all but certain that he suffered martyrdom under Nero. The author of Luke-Acts tends to put the Roman government in a favorable light. Perhaps he did not want to recount the Neronian atrocities. The suggestion that Luke planned a third volume is of course pure speculation.

If Luke did write as early as Nero, Mark would have to be

---

[4] Statement made to a class.

dated as early as 60, which would be inconsistent with the inclusion of the chapter on the destruction of Jerusalem. Some have thought Luke used the writings of Josephus, which would bring his own work down near 100. Somewhere near 80 seems more probable.

Polycarp, in the middle of the second century, writing to the Philippians, in 2.1, loosely quotes Acts 2:24. Marcion, the mid-century advocate of discarding the Old Testament, used Luke as the only Gospel in his Christian bible. Not much later Tatian compiled a composite Gospel from the materials of the Four. From these facts we know that Luke was in circulation in the middle of the second century. However, it was the last of the four Gospels to be mentioned by name. This was toward the end of the century and by Irenaeus, Greek bishop of Lyon, in his work, Against Heresies, 3.1. It is possible the ascription of Luke's name to the Gospel was an inference from Paul's statements in Colossians and Philemon.

The primary interest of Acts is the growth and spread of the Christian movement. This is stated by the author in his preface. At the very beginning of the train of events that eventually spread "throughout all Judea and Samaria, and to the ends of the earth," was the birth of John the Baptist, with which Luke's first volume opens. The second closes with the gospel established at Rome, after tracing the progress in Syria, Asia Minor, and Greece.

STRUCTURE OF ACTS

In examining the structure of the second volume one finds a number of landmarks and threads of interest. One major feature is the shift from the Jewish to the gentile mission, from Palestine and Syria to countries along the northern Mediterranean, from Peter to Paul. Hellenized Jews were the link by which the shift was made. In this transfer of interest one passes out of the realm of miracle and legend into an atmosphere of fact and eyewitness reports. This difference reflects the author's background, apparently not Palestinian.

It is a striking fact that the Greek style of the earlier part of

Acts differs from the latter part of the book.[5] Statistical studies, computerized and otherwise, of linguistic features of New Testament writings seem usually to confirm views developed many years previously on other grounds.

The interests of the author of Acts are indicated by certain formulas, e.g., "they were adhering steadfastly to the teaching of the apostles, to the fellowship, to the breaking of bread, and to prayers," 1:14, 2:42, and 6:4; "The Lord was adding daily to the saved," 2:47, 5:14, 6:1, 7, 11:24; "and there were added on that day about three thousand souls," 2:41 and 4:4; "and great fear came on all who heard," 2:43, 5:5, 11; "And the word of God increased," 6:7, 12:24, and 19:20.

Other main features are the sermons put in the mouth of Peter, Stephen, and Paul. These are particularly valuable as showing dominant interests of Christian preachers in the last half of the first century.

The outline of Paul's journeys was discussed in the preceding chapter.

In his Gospel Luke often copies Mark with less revision than Matthew makes, but the material compiled in Acts may have been used with more freedom, the traditions being less sacred and fixed. At any rate the language seems less colloquial. Yet sometimes in the Gospel Luke adopts literary expressions distinctly more learned than those of the other evangelists.

The "we" section of Acts are discussed in the previous chapter, page 30.

LUKE AS A HISTORIAN

Although the title has been given to another, Luke deserves to be known as the father of church history. This in spite of the fact that some say he was no historian at all. In evaluating his work it may be observed that he specifically recognized the superiority of eyewitness reports; that he had historical imagination, noting some of the lacunae in previous work and attempting to fill them; that he is the only New Testament

---

[5] Cf. R. A. Martin, "Syntactical Evidence of Aramaic Sources in Acts I-XV," *New Testament Studies,* Vol. 10, No. 1, Oct. 1964.

writer who makes a serious attempt to fix the date of the birth of Jesus; that he supplies a final separation of Jesus and the apostles; that he rationalizes the order of the temptation incidents; that he seems to have followed his critical inclinations in omitting a considerable part of Mark after the feeding of the five thousand; and to have used primary sources when they were available, as in the we sections of Acts. In all these matters he seems to have adopted what appeared to him the most probable solution, which is all that can be demanded of a historian writing for the general public. He was a man of his time in attitudes toward ghosts and miracles, and in his concept of the structure of the universe. As noted before, he treated Marcan quotations more carefully than Matthew did, giving them with less revision. We may suppose this was true of his handling of Q and other sources.

His history of course is history with a purpose, i.e., his primary object being the promotion of the Christian faith.

5. John

John is the most popular of the Gospels. This is no doubt due to its superior capacity for creating a devotional atmosphere. With practically no interest in ethics, and only incidental interest in history, it is the supreme devotional work of the New Testament.

To understand the devotional power of the book one should contemplate such passages as Nicodemus' interview; the Samaritan woman, 4:1-42; the vine and the branches, as well as other farewell discourses in chapters 14-17. The repetition and restatement have a cumulative effect that is inescapable.

The most popular and easiest expression of religion is prayer, together with other customary exercises in public and private worship. The most difficult expression of religion is constant, consistent loving-kindness to all fellow creatures. This warm ethical concern for the welfare of others is clearly enjoined in each of the Synoptic Gospels, in Paul's letters, and in James. It is hardly mentioned in the Fourth Gospel.

The love of the Fourth Gospel is a love within the closely-knit mystic fellowship of the religious group, the love of the members for each other and for Christ, the love of Christ for the fellowship and for his divine Father. Love for the supreme deity on the part of man is an abstraction hardly attempted; but deity is brought down to earth and localized, visualized in the person of Christ. On the other hand, the humanity of Jesus is to a considerable extent lost. In this Gospel we but dimly perceive Jesus of Nazareth. He has been transformed into the Christ of God.

When this Gospel was written, Christianity had acquired its catholic and essential character. It was already far removed from Judaism. Gentiles could no longer call its members atheists, for they now had a visible and tangible god, localized first in the imagination, next in the sacrament of his body and blood, and ready for his artistic representation in painting, mosaic, and sculpture, all of which flourished in substantial form as soon as the new religion was legalized.

Nevertheless, it is of the genius of catholic Christianity never to have completely lost the most primitive traces of its origin. This can be more plainly seen in the Fourth Gospel than anywhere else in the New Testament. While representing Christ as incarnate deity, it makes the bald statement that Jesus is the son of Joseph, 1:45, 6:42; while making a more or less tangible, localized Christ the focus of devotion, it alone clearly states that God is a spirit, 4:24, and that those who worship him must do so in spirit and truth; while treating Jews as a people apart, even from Jesus, it alone reminds the Church with inescapable clarity, that "salvation is from the Jews," 4:22.

Mysticism was in the ascendancy in the Hellenistic world. Even Judaism, before the beginning of Christianity, was strongly influenced by Greek mysticism. The Judaism that flourished beyond the confines of Palestine contributed to its mysticism, as well as to other features of the primitive Church. The Church however did not stop with the mysticism inherited from the Synagog, but absorbed more and more along with its converts from paganism. So one should expect the least Palestinian and most Greek of the Gospels to be full of mysticism. Especially impressive mystic passages are the interview with Nicodemus, with its doctrine of the new birth, 3:1-21; the parable of the vine and the branches, 15:1-16, picturesquely expressing the Pauline doctrine of union with Christ; and the sacramental sermon on eating Christ's body and drinking his blood, 6:31-59.

The strong sacramental background of the Fourth Gospel is not always recognized. It is instructive to observe Protestant ministers, at least those of the non-immersionist denominations, how they ignore the word *water*, when reading and discussing Nicodemus' interview with Jesus, 3:1-21, and the statement about the new birth, 3:5. Likewise in handling the discourse on the bread of life, 6:26 ff., they usually, if not always, ignore verses 53-54, which Catholics of course emphasize. Taken at face value they teach transubstantiation, for Jesus says we cannot have eternal life unless we eat his flesh and drink his blood.

AUTHOR AND DATE

The Fourth Gospel and traditional Christianity in general are most vulnerable when investigated by the methods of historical research. Since the end of the second century Christendom generally has taken for granted that this Gospel was written at Ephesus by John, the son of Zebedee, the beloved disciple who reclined next to Jesus at the Last Supper.

Irenaeus, bishop of Lyon, writing toward the end of the second century, made a desperate effort to establish this view. Christendom was easy to convince, for it wanted to believe the very best about this book. Irenaeus says, Against Heresies 3.3.4, that he remembers listening to Polycarp at Ephesus when he himself was a small boy, and that Polycarp spoke of association with John and others who had seen the Lord. Careful reading of all extant statements by Irenaeus shows that, try as he would, he could not remember anything definite about John. We conclude he did not succeed in forging the link he so strongly desired. Even if John did teach at Ephesus, that does not prove he wrote the Gospel. Cf. also the fragment quoted by Eusebius, Church History, 5.20.4-6.

The traditional belief in the long life of John may have been produced by the desire to justify the earlier conviction that the second coming of Christ would take place while some of the disciples were still living. At least two ancient writers state that John did not live to a great age. Clement of Alexandria in Stromata 7.17 says the teaching of the apostles, including the ministry of Paul, was completed under Nero, Clement being little if any later than Irenaeus. Mark 10:39 promises martyrdom to James and John. We know James was put to death under Herod Agrippa I in the year 44, Acts 12:1-2. There are indications John also suffered at an early date, though there is no reliable and definite report of his death. Papias wrote that it was at the hands of the Jews.

Tatian used all four Gospels in his Diatessaron shortly after the middle of the second century, so must have regarded John as Scripture. Justin Martyr, writing very little earlier, apparently does not regard it as Scripture, for he quotes it only once, and then not by name, though his writing is voluminous and his use of Scripture extensive. His work may be dated as early as 140. No earlier use of the Fourth Gospel has been demonstrated.

Two significant accompanying circumstances must be noted in connexion with Justin's one allusion, and his failure to mention the book by name: first, he quotes and uses the Synoptic Gospels; second, he uses and names the Apocalypse, regarding it as the work of John the apostle. From these considerations it seems certain Justin did not consider the Fourth Gospel the work of the apostle, the son of Zebedee.

The fact that Marcion chose Luke instead of John demands an explanation. John seems more in harmony with Marcion's special interests. So it can be inferred he did not regard this Gospel as apostolic.

The earliest writer to refer to it by name is Theophilus of Antioch, who wrote in the last quarter of the second century, being only slightly earlier than Irenaeus.

No definite date can be given for the writing of John. It must have been between 90 and 130. Tradition always placed its composition near the year 100. There is no convincing argument for disputing such a date; but the fathers of the first half of the second century certainly would have used it had they believed the son of Zebedee the author.

This Gospel begins with a philosophical prologue, some of its concepts no longer meaningful. The first half of the book contains incidents of a somewhat general public ministry of Jesus, the second half giving incidents of the Passion Week. The last chapter is an appendix adding a Galilean appearance of the risen Lord to the previously given Jerusalem appearances.

Except in this broad general way, little attention is paid to chronological arrangement. The expulsion of commerce from the Temple is in the second chapter, at the beginning of the public ministry, instead of near the end as the Synoptics have it. Two Passover trips are given, and between them a "holiday" trip, all to Jerusalem. The Synoptics have only one adult trip to Jerusalem. John's first Passover trip is in the second chapter. Throughout the fifth chapter he is on the holiday trip, teaching in Jerusalem. But suddenly, in the opening sentence of the sixth chapter, he is crossing the Lake in Galilee. The second Passover trip is in the seventh chapter. He does not return to Galilee until after his resurrection, and then only in the appendix, chapter twenty-one. Eight or nine months after this second Passover he is still in Jerusalem, teaching in Solomon's porch at the time of the feast of Dedication, having been there through the festival of Booths. Immediately after the December scene comes the raising of Lazarus and the beginning of the Passion Week, i.e., about the first week of April. He is therefore depicted as being in Jerusalem from one Passover till the next, whereas in the Synoptics he spends only his final week in Jerusalem. It is doubtful whether the author was concerned with such questions.

The Fourth Gospel shows a fondness for threes, as pointed out by B. W. Bacon, referring to H. Holtzmann. There are three of each of the following: propositions in the prologue, days spent with the Baptist, times Jesus was in Galilee, journeys to Judea, Passovers, other feasts, mighty works in Judea, mighty works in Galilee, divisions of the discourse on the last day of Booths, disclosures of the traitor, times Jesus was condemned, times Pilate tries to save him, words spoken on the Cross, days in the tomb, and appearances to the disciples.[7]

Repetition is an important factor in the effect of the book. Ideas are repeated time and again in language of childlike simplicity till a spell is cast over the reader or hearer, and he cannot fail to grasp the point. The language has some modern flavor and is the easiest in the New Testament for a present-day Greek to read.

No literary sources can be identified except Mark and Luke, both treated with the utmost freedom, e.g., the position of the passages on the expulsion of commerce from the Temple, the omission of eschatology and exorcism, and the rewording of Synoptic incidents. He does not copy as they do. "The only Synoptic writer from whom he quotes verbatim is Mark, and that quite rarely," [8] though he seems to depend on Mark in a number of passages, which may be listed as follows:

baptism with water, 1:26-27, Mk. 1:7-8
expulsion of commerce, 2:13-22, Mk. 11:15-19
feeding 5,000, fragments in "baskets," 6:1-14, Mk. 6:30-44
walking on water, 6:16-21, Mk. 6:45-52 (not in Lk.)
anointing by Mary of Bethany, 12:1-8, Mk. 14:3-9 (identification)
triumphal entry, 12:12-19, Mk. 11:1-11 (disagrees with Mt.)
prophecy of denial, 13:36-38, Mk. 14:27-31 (Mt., Lk., Jn. omit "twice.")
betrayal and arrest, 18:1-12, Mk. 14:43-52 (Jn. and Lk. have "right ear." Jn. names high priest's slave and omits Judas' kiss.)
denial, 18:25-27, Mk. 14:66-72
custom of release at Passover, 18:39, Mk. 15:6 (Lk. omits.)
scourged and mocked, 19:1-3, Mk. 15:16-19 (Lk. omits.)
arrival at Golgotha, 19:17b, Mk. 15:22

The last chapter of the book is obviously an appendix, the end of the twentieth chapter being the original conclusion. In the appendix Peter is restored to favor, there is belated men-

---

[7] Bacon, B. W. *An Introduction to the New Testament*, p. 253.
[8] Bacon, *The Fourth Gospel in Research and Debate*, p. 367.

tion of the sons of Zebedee, and an attempt to identify the main author with the disciple Jesus loved, though he is not even here mentioned by name. The mysterious Nathanael appears again in the appendix, and Galilean appearances of the risen Lord harmonize with Mark and Matthew. Otherwise John gives Jerusalem appearances in agreement with Luke.

An especially curious feature of the Appendix is the number of fish caught. Jerome, in his commentary on Ezekiel 47, Migne xxv, 594-5, gives an ancient statement that the total species of fish are 153.[9] However, this statement has not been found. Pliny the Elder, *Natural History* 9.16 and 32.53, gives some comparably low estimates. Anyhow, it seems the sort of device the writer of the Fourth Gospel would employ to suggest that the seine "gathered of every kind."

There is no evidence that the Gospel ever circulated without the appendix, except for the negative indication of the middle-sized appendix to Mark, which uses Johannine resurrection material, but none from the appendix.

CHRISTOLOGY

This writer, like Paul in First Corinthians 8:6 and Colossians 1:16, identifies the pre-existent Christ as the acting agent in creation. This doctrine of a distinct divine being, associated with the supreme God, is found in pre-Christian Jewish Wisdom literature, e.g., Proverbs 8, Wisdom of Solomon 7:22 ff., and Wisdom of Sirach 24. There is also a striking figurative passage in Plato's Republic 6.508. B-C, "This is he whom I call the son of the Good, whom the Good begot to be in the visible world, analogous to himself in the mental realm." Paul clearly expresses the idea in Philippians 2:6-11, that a preexistent divine being came to earth and inhabited a human body. In contrast to the Synoptics the Fourth Gospel takes this Pauline view, presenting a Christology of incarnation. Jesus is not a man who became God, but God who became man. "The Word became flesh and lived among us," John 1:14.

Of Gospel tradition in general it may be said that, as it

---

[9] Jerome here confuses John 21:6 with Luke 5:6.

progressed, it made Jesus more and more divine and less and less human. This drift can be seen in the Synoptics, but is more advanced in the Fourth, not because of a later date, but because of different local tradition.

In the Fourth Gospel Jesus has fewer human traits: a curtain is drawn across the humiliating scene of baptism by a mere man; the temptation is ignored; there is no weariness, hunger, or pain, no agony in Gethsemane, no kiss by the foul lips of Judas, nor is he spit on by the Roman executioners; he bears his own cross and gives up his life voluntarily for the purpose of fulfilling prophecy and providing redemption. It is even more evident than in Paul and the Synoptics that the author is not interested in the life of Jesus of Nazareth, but in painting a picture of the Messiah Savior. The purpose of this Gospel is stated at the close of the main body of the work, 20:31, "These things are written so you may believe Jesus is the Christ, and that by believing you may have life in his name."

The book is far less Jewish than the Synoptics and far more Greek. The word "Jews" is used sixty-eight times, while the Synoptics use it only five or six times apiece. It is one of the striking non-Palestinian features. Jews are spoken of as if Jesus were not one. He told the Jews they could not come where he was going. The anachronism of such passages is fairly obvious. Christian preachers in gentile environments composed imaginary discourses of what they believed Jesus must have said.

Not only do such compositions reveal the anachronism of the writer, but sometimes they display positive irrationality, as when a crowd responds, 12:34, in unison with a thirty word doctrinal challenge, and when the crowd asks for a sign immediately after the feeding of the five thousand. There is an unmistakable anachronism in 11:55, where the writer speaks of the "Passover of the Jews." Any reader might well ask, "What other Passover was there in the days of Jesus?" Only after the Church was a going concern was it necessary to distinguish in Greek between the Christian *pascha* and the Jewish *pascha,* for Easter and Passover were, and still are, the same word in Greek. One of the most absurd passages in this Gospel is the question, 9:2, "Did this man sin, or his parents, that he was born blind?"

Like most present day Christians, the writer is usually unmindful of the fact that Jesus was a Jew, but it is recalled when the context requires, as in the dialogue with the Samaritan woman in chapter 4.

Christianity has been mainly a way of worshipping, but has never entirely abandoned the Jewish principle that religion should be a way of living. Greek philosophy helped preserve the ethical note, which, it must be admitted, has always labored under difficulties, often dying to the merest whisper. Now and then there have been spurts of intellectual activity bringing criticism of the superstitious credulities and inconsistencies into which society continually drifts. Furthermore, Christianity has always been a brotherhood, ministering to social instincts. The persistent, subordinate ethical element has kept alive a certain amount of interest in Matthew and Luke; but the all-pervading devotional spirit has always found its favorite expression in John.

Modern intellectual awakening has applied the methods of historical research to first one and then another part of the Bible, and to Christian tradition in general. The results have been more disturbing with regard to John than with any other book of the New Testament. The historian believes he gets a less imaginative picture of Jesus in Mark. Those who are interested in ethics find their greatest interest in Matthew and Luke.

CHAPTER IV

Apocalyptic Writings

The apocalypses form a literary tradition of dreams, dreams that often became lurid, that were full of terror, by authors under strong emotional pressure, writing for people whose very lives were at stake, and who could see no honorable escape from the suffering and destruction that confronted them. This literary tradition had its beginnings in the tragedies of Jewish history.

First Israel had fallen under the Assyrians and then Judah was destroyed by the Babylonians. Years afterward, under the benevolent rule of Cyrus the Persian, they began to rebuild Jerusalem. The process was slow and painful. They were bitterly oppressed by later Persian rulers. They were continually at the mercy of the great world powers, who marched their armies mercilessly back and forth through Palestine. Pious souls and deathless spirits, steeled to endure any atrocity rather than conform to the dictates of brute force, found their only consolation in sublime faith that the Lord God omnipotent reigns, even if all's wrong on the earth. If this were true, then they had to believe that he would one day overwhelm the wicked and drive them from the face of the earth. At the same time he would reward the righteous with a golden era of peace, plenty, and joy.

Traces of such convictions are found in all the Old Testament prophets, but became dominant in Ezekiel, Zechariah, Daniel, Enoch, and the Sibylline Oracles. Somewhat similar interests may be seen in certain pagan classics, such as the eleventh book of the Odyssey, where Odysseus visits the realm of the departed;

the sixth book of the Aeneid, with its reworking of the same theme; and the much quoted passage from Vergil's Fourth Eclogue, which is almost a prophecy of the Messiah.

> *Now is come the last age of the song of Cumae;*
> *The great line of the centuries begins anew.*
> *Now the Virgin returns, the reign of Saturn returns;*
> *Now a new generation descends from heaven on high.*
> *Only do thou, pure Lucina, smile on the birth of the child,*
> *Under whom the iron brood shall first cease,*
> *And a golden race spring up anew throughout the world![1]*

1. The Revelation of John

The finest flower of apocalyptic literature is the Revelation of John, the only apocalypse to find a place in the New Testament.

There is something inescapably Byzantine about the New Testament Apocalypse. One acquainted with the Eastern Orthodox Church can hardly read this book without being reminded of it. The Apocalypse seems to have furnished Eastern Christians with the ideal vision they strove to express in their buildings and ritual. It may be nearer the truth to say the same oriental splendors that formed the environment of this writer were also factors in the development of the Byzantine liturgies.

First among the characteristic features of Orthodox public worship may be mentioned the chanting, either the weird Byzantine psaltery, or the exquisite Russian harmonies. The Apocalypse is a book of chants, e.g., "You are worthy, O Lord, to take the book, and to open its seals, for you were slaughtered, and with your blood have redeemed for God men out of every tribe and language and people and nation, and you have made them a kingdom and priests for our God, and they will rule on the earth."

"Worthy is the Lamb that was slaughtered to take the power and wealth and wisdom and might and honor and glory and blessing."

---

[1] Translation by H. R. Fairclough, Loeb Classics, ad loc. Heinemann, London, 1916; Now Harvard University Press.

"Holy, holy, holy, Lord God almighty, who were and are, and are to come."

"To him who is seated on the throne and to the Lamb, be blessing and honor and power forever and ever."

"Salvation to our God who is sitting on the throne, and to the Lamb."

"Amen! The blessing and the glory and the wisdom and the thanks and the honor and the power and the might be to our God forever and ever."

And so the chants continue throughout the book, but there are other features no less reminiscent of Orthodoxy. The all-pervading smell of incense is recalled by the words of the Apocalypse, "The four animals and the twenty-four elders fell down before the Lamb, each with a harp and golden bowls full of incense, which are the prayers of the saints."

The Orthodox sanctuary is full of candles or electric lights, reminding one of the seven golden lampstands among which John saw a son of man in glittering raiment with eyes like flames of fire.

Orthodox churches are full of color and ornaments, and we find in the Apocalypse brass, white wool, fire, gold, stars, rainbows, black, red, white, and pale green horses, precious stones such as jasper, sapphires, chalcedony, emerald, sardonyx, sardius, chrysolite, beryl, topaz, chrysoprase, jacynth, and amethyst; there are seas of glass and crystal; transparent gold and a final burst of glory in which it is declared that the holy city, the new Jerusalem, has no need of the sun or moon to light it, for the Lord God and the Lamb are its light. The bright vestments of Orthodox clergy are more than matched by the woman whom the seer sees dressed in the sun. Because the book is so vivid, and its vocabulary and sentences so simple, it is easy for a beginner to read. With easy words it evokes a vision in technicolor.

Like the Orthodox rituals the book is full of dramatic action, and just as interest is maintained in the liturgy, even when one does not understand the language, so the vivid action of the Apocalypse makes it readable, even for those who completely misunderstand its purpose. In the liturgy there are processions, the little and great entrances, much moving about of the clergy and acolytes, members of the congregation are in motion kissing icons, lighting candles, making the sign of the cross, while little children often run about in the back of the church. And what action there is in the Apocalypse! Horses and riders go out to war, angels are seen flying, a great dragon pursues a woman and she is given the wings of an eagle and flies away into the desert, seven bowls of wrath are poured out on the earth, beasts come up out of the earth and out of the sea, the armies of good and evil are arrayed for the greatest of all world wars, there are earthquakes, the sun and moon are convulsed, the sky is rolled up like a scroll, and after all these mighty upheavals the holy city, even the new Jerusalem, comes down out of heaven like a bride adorned for her husband.

Beside all this there is a note of savagery in the book that is perhaps more Byzantine than Orthodox. There are barbaric chants gloating over the destruction of Rome; "God has remembered her injustices . . . reward her as she has rewarded others, and make her punishment twice as heavy as her deeds . . . give her torture and grief . . . death, torture, and famine, and let her be consumed with fire!" Great choruses of kings, merchants, tradesmen, and sailors, each in turn, lament over the fall of Rome as they stand about the burning city; and then the vindictive chant, "Gloat over her, heaven and saints and apostles and prophets, because God has exacted your revenge from her." These attitudes are in the character of the sons of Zebedee, as they appear in Luke's central portion, where they want to call down fire from heaven and destroy the Samaritans; but they are not in the spirit of the Sermon on the Mount.

The Apocalypse is a masterpiece of impressionistic art, something to be felt rather than to be talked about. The imagery is fantastic, sometimes reminding one of passages in Lucian.

STRUCTURE

The book is a mosaic, made up largely of words, pictures, phrases, and ideas taken from other prophetic and apocalyptic literature. It quotes the Old Testament far more than does any other book of the New Testament.

The letters to the seven churches, in the second and third chapters, are apparently modeled after the prophecies to the seven nations, with which the book of Amos opens,[2] the throne surrounded by a rainbow and set on a sea of glass is taken from the first chapter of Ezekiel, as are also the four mystic animals; the trisagion is from the sixth chapter of Isaiah; from Zechariah come the riders on colored horses and the two olive trees standing by the Lord of all the earth; and so on through more than two hundred borrowings from the Old Testament.

The number seven plays a prominent part. There are the following seven sevens: seven letters to seven churches, seven angels, seven seals, seven plagues, and seven kings of the seven-hilled city. The letters, seals, and angels are occupied with judgments, portents, and prophecies of doom. Such items constitute the bulk of the book. Then come the executions of judgment, followed by a new sky and a new earth, when the new Jerusalem comes down from the sky, inaugurating the messianic reign on earth.

DATE AND AUTHOR

The purpose of the book is to give comfort and hope to Christians suffering for their faith at the hand of the Roman empire. This at once raises the question, Who was the emperor? Many who have examined the problem think the book was written toward the end of the reign of Domitian, but there have always been those who argued for the time of Nero.

It is known that a number of Christians suffered horrible deaths under Nero, but apparently it was not because the government had begun at that early date definitely to oppose Christianity. The story told by Tacitus in Annals 15.44 is that Nero was looking for scapegoats after the great fire, which he was accused of setting. The Christians were an insignificant and despised minority, so could be sacrificed with impunity. The

---

[2] J. M. Rife, "The Literary Background of Revelation II-III." *Journal of Biblical Literature*, LX, II. 1941.

affair was local and personal. In contrast to this, Revelation evidences a general persecution in Asia Minor.

Nero is first on the traditional list of persecuting emperors, next come Domitian and Trajan. Eusebius, in 3.17, 20, 33 of his Church History, begins with these three, but seems to absolve Trajan of personal responsibility. Tertullian, in chapter 5 of his Apology, limits deliberate hostility to the first two, and says Domitian was "a very Nero for cruelty." There are two statements in Revelation that refer specifically to an emperor, but they are in symbolical language of uncertain interpretation. First is 13:18, in which the number of the man is said to be 666. Irenaeus discusses the meaning of this number on the supposition that it refers to a name in Greek letters. Both Hebrew and Greek use letters of the alphabet as numerals.

The number 666 in this passage was likely obtained by adding the numerical value of the Hebrew letters spelling Neron Caesar in Hebrew, viz., *nrwn qsr* (n=50, r=200, w=6, q=100, s=60). The Greek form of the name is Neron, the Latin Nero. Lacking one *n*, the Latin form adds up to 616. This is an ancient textual variant known to Irenaeus, but not understood by him, mentioned in his work Against Heresies, 5.30. The fact that both numbers are perfectly intelligible on the basis of the Hebrew, when applied respectively to the Greek and Latin spellings of Nero when transliterated into Hebrew, can hardly be coincidence. These facts agree too with the barbarous character of the Greek in the Apocalypse. Nothing would be more natural than for a native speaker of Aramaic to resort to the Hebrew numerical system when he wanted to conceal the meaning. It would have been too easy in Greek. I conclude the number certainly stands for Nero.

Now comes a greater difficulty. Can Nero be a symbol for some later emperor, particularly Domitian? Tertullian says Domitian was "a very Nero for cruelty." There was a superstition that Nero was to rise from the dead to further plague humanity. In Revelation 17:10-11 we read, "There are seven kings; five have fallen, one is, the other has not yet come. And when he comes it is necessary for him to remain awhile. And the beast that was and is not, he himself is the eighth and is among the seven." This last statement seems to refer to the risen Nero, but we are not sure how to count the emperors. Some ancient writers count Julius Caesar first. Clement of Alexandria in Stromateis 1.21 gives two lists, one beginning with Julius and the other with Augustus. In the latter Nero is fifth, Vespasian seventh, and Titus eighth. This still leaves Domitian out of the picture. A Jewish writer may well have seen Titus, the destroyer of Jerusalem and the Temple, as Nero come to life again. Some think we have here a Jewish text imperfectly adapted to its place in the Christian mosaic. Although the Jewish writer may have referred to Titus, the Christian borrower may have thought Domitian fitted the description better. Irenaeus, Against Heresies 5.30.4, says Revelation is Domitianic. Many modern scholars would agree, but no definite proof seems possible. The author no doubt intended this to be so.

The traditional view that the author was the Apostle John was first stated explicitly by Justin, Dialog 81.4. The Domitianic date is first given by Irenaeus. If any book in the New Testament was written by one whose mother tongue was Aramaic, this must be it; and if any of the five Johannine books was written by the son of Zebedee, it must be this. The greatest objection to this view is the alleged previous martyrdom of John. One of the Papias fragments says, "He was killed by the Jews, having fulfilled, together with his brother, Christ's prophecy that they would drink the cup he was drinking." George Hamartolos, who reports the passage,[4] believes the martyrdoms happened after the writing of the Apocalypse. His ninth century opinion has less weight than his quotation from Papias, though with Papias too it was only hearsay. Its correctness is indicated by its contradiction of the prevalent belief of the Church. Its survival in spite of this gives it a certain weight.

Papias, Justin, and Irenaeus were all admirers of the Apocalypse and thus inclined to grant it apostolic authority. Irenaeus shut his eyes to the difference in the Greek of the Apocalypse and the Fourth Gospel, stoutly supporting the Johannine authorship of both. Justin regarded the Apocalypse as Johannine, but not the Gospel. Papias thought the author

---

4 Papiae fragmentum XI, Gebhardt, Harnack & Zahn, Patrum apostolicorum opera, ed. 6, minor. Leipzig 1920.

of the Apocalypse was John, but does not seem to have known the Gospel.

Eusebius was one of the many who have not liked the Apocalypse. He attempted to undermine its apostolic authority, pointing out, Church History 7.25, an earlier observation on the difference in language between it and the Gospel. This difference has been unknown to most Christians because they have not read it in Greek. Reading a translation, admirers of the book are not reminded of the language and objectors are deprived of their strongest internal argument.

The historical student finds it easier to think of John the son of Zebedee as the author of Revelation than of the Gospel. He finds it all but impossible to regard both as the work of the same man. He hardly sees how the son of Zebedee could have written either.

2. THE SHEPHERD

AUTHOR

"The man who raised me sold me to a woman in Rome by the name of Rose."

Who ever put more autobiography into one line? These opening words of the Shepherd, showing Roman civilization at its worst, plainly imply that Hermas, the author, had been exposed by his parents, that he had been picked up by a foundling farmer and raised for the slave market.

There is more truth than we like to believe in the legends of Oedipus, Moses, Cyrus the Great, Romulus and Remus, how as infants they were exposed to be found by someone or to die. One Greek papyrus letter, written by a soldier to his wife in Egypt, says, "If the child (to be born) is a boy, keep him. If it is a girl, throw her out." Another bit of papyrus correspondence concerns a newborn boy a foundling a farmer found on a dunghill. He farmed the boy out with a wet nurse who had a son of the same age as the foundling. One of the boys died. The foundling farmer took the survivor away, claiming the nurse's son had died. She then got the child away from the slave trader and he brought suit for recovery. It is against such a background that we are to read Hermas' opening line.

From other remarks in the Shepherd we gather that Hermas was a freedman at the time of writing, Visions 1.1.2; that he had a small business of some sort, Vis. 2.3,3.1; that he had a financial reverse, Vis. 3.6.7; that he did not get along well either with his wife or children, Vis. 1.2, 2.3, Parable 7.2; that his wife was at first not a Christian, Vis. 2.2.3; that he was an active as well as ambitious member of the Roman church, Vis. 1.1, 2.4; that he wanted to be one of the church officers that sat on the most honorable section of the front seat, Vis. 3.1; that he was tired of having his ambition thwarted, Vis. 3.1.9; and that he hoped the Shepherd would attain the dignity of being read in church, Vis. 2.4.3. He was so successful that his book, the longest of the Apostolic Fathers, was considered Scripture by many ancient Christians. It is part of the New Testament in Codex Sinaiticus.

DATE

The Greek of the Shepherd is simple and unpretentious, somewhat more simple and modern sounding than John. Dr. Procope Costas, once in a conversation, compared it to the language of a newspaper. It should be added however that the literary Greek of most newspapers of that date would not have tolerated some of Hermas' colloquialisms.

Estimates of the date of the book have varied from the end of the first century to the middle of the second. Reasons for preferring the earlier date are the colloquial language, the unconventional portrait of Christ (?), reference to a Christian meeting as a synagogue in Commandments 11, the instruction to give a copy of the book to Clement so he could send it to other cities, Vis. 2.4.3, and the primitive list of officials in Vis. 3.5.1. The later books of the New Testament speak of bishops, elders (priests), and deacons. Not so Hermas and Paul. Those who date the book later argue for an expansion of the original by a later writer.

The book consists of five visions, twelve commandments, and ten parables revealed to the author during ecstatic experiences. In the first few a woman appears to him and communicates messages. She is sometimes said to be the Church. In the rest of the book it is a man dressed like a shepherd who makes the revelations. Sometimes he is called the angel of repentance.

I suspect the shepherd, at least in his earlier appearances, is the good Shepherd himself, though students of the book have not, to my knowledge, suggested this identification. There are obvious reasons in some of the Parables why such an identification may be rejected.

If the identification and date are correct, we have here a portrait of Christ in the mind of a late first century Roman Christian: "glorious in appearance, dressed like a shepherd, a white skin thrown about him, having a bag on his shoulder and a staff in his hand," Vis. 5.1.1.

CHARACTER

The words Jesus and Christ do not appear once in the entire book. This is in marked contrast to the other Apostolic Fathers. In the Parables, however, the phrase "the son of God" occurs twenty-nine times, mostly in the ninth Parable. Moreover, in these passages he is distinct from the angel of repentance. This may be some more of Hermas' inconsistency. The most striking example of this is in Par. 9.1.1, where he says, "the holy spirit which spoke to you in the form of the Church is the son of God."

These and other inconsistencies may be due, not to duality or multiplicity of authorship, but to confusion in Hermas' thinking. One nice example of this is in Vis. 3.8.5, where he says seven women who have appeared are "daughters of one another," reminding one of the nursery rhyme about the snake that swallows itself.

The uniform character of the Greek indicates the work of one man.

As implied above, the Shepherd is the work of a naive mind, whose style is rambling, confused, and often tiresome, more tiresome the further he goes. It is characteristic of him that he would leave some doubt in the reader's mind as to just who the angel of repentance is.

He sometimes sounds as if he had heard the Bible read in church, but had no copy of his own to consult, e.g., Parable 5.5.

One of the most overdone passages is the eighth Parable, in which he attempts to show how far a Christian can go in sin without being lost. He strings out a dozen different degrees of faithfulness and unfaithfulness, symbolized by sticks cut from a willow tree by the angel Michael. He passes these out to people who later bring the sticks back for his judgment. The angel then arranges the sticks in twelve different piles, according to the twelve different conditions in which he finds them, some dried up, some green, some sprouted, etc., etc., ad nauseam.

One can only applaud the good sense of the Christian public, which, though using and valuing the Shepherd for at least three centuries, finally relegated it to practical oblivion. It constitutes 40% of the total bulk of the Apostolic Fathers, growing duller and more confused as it progresses, though the opening pages are rather interesting.

SPECIAL INTERESTS

The book is largely concerned with repentance, first with the problem of reinstating those who have lapsed during persecution, and then in general with the problem of how heinously a baptized person can sin without perishing everlastingly. The solutions are a jumble of not always consistent compromises. In Commandment 4.3. he says there is no forgiveness of post-baptismal sins, but there is one more chance after yielding to severe temptation. Throughout the book there is evidence on the early stages of the sacrament of penance. Blasphemy and betrayal are the two unpardonable sins. Martyrdom is prominent as a major virtue. These features seem to fit the view that the book was begun soon after the persecution under the emperor Domitian.

There are frequent lists of virtues and vices, reminding one of similar lists in Paul's writings, and in those of other Hellenistic moralists.

111

The theology is primitive. The term literally translated "Holy Spirit" seems to mean "a spirit of holiness," i.e., does not personify or deify the concept in a Trinitarian sense. He speaks in Commandment 10.3.2 of the "cheerful holy spirit that has been given to man," and, Commandment 10.3.3, of "sadness mixed with the holy spirit."

Falling from grace is everywhere taken for granted, e.g., Commandment 9.9. A common phrase is "live for God." In Commandment 5.1.5 the verb "he was embittered" is apparently another bit of early Christian lingo that became crystallized in worship, viz., in the curiously repeated *epikranthe* response near the end of the Greek Orthodox Easter service during the reading of a selection from a sermon of John Chrysostom.

There are curious allusions to certain New Testament passages. In Commandment 4.1.4-6 he gives the Roman rule on divorce; in 12.5.2 the advice to "resist the devil and he will flee from you," occurring also in James, was probably a common saying in the early church. The repeated reference in Commandment 11. to a Christian meeting as a synagogue, is also reminiscent of James. The false prophet wanting pay, Commandment 11.12, reminds one of the Didache and Ignatius. "Prophesying in a corner," Commandment 11.13, is a figure occurring in Acts 26:26. And the spiritual armor of Commandment 12.2.4-5 and Ephesians 6:11-17 are borrowed from Isaiah. All of the above were no doubt common Christian sayings at the turn of the century.

In Commandment 11.20 there is a reference to "the drop of water that falls from the tile and bores a hole in the stone."

No complete manuscript of the Greek text of the Shepherd has survived, as far as is known. Codex Sinaiticus contains the first fourth, i.e., to Commandment 4.3.6; a nearly complete manuscript of the 14th or 15th century was found over a century ago in a monastery on Mt. Athos, but it lacks the last part of the 9th Parable and all of the 10th; the University of Michigan has 25 leaves of a 4th century papyrus manuscript containing Parable 2.8-9.5.2; and numerous papyrus fragments have been identified. Many manuscripts of Latin translations are known. A manuscript of an Ethiopic translation was discovered

112

in 1847 in an Ethiopian monastery. Also fragments of a Coptic version have been found in Egypt.

3. The Revelation of Peter

A small New Testament could be assembled of works ascribed to Peter. It would contain each of the four types of writing found in the New Testament, for there is a Gospel of Peter, an Acts of Peter, two letters of Peter, and a Revelation of Peter. At various times and places each of these five books has been regarded as the work of Peter, though he probably wrote none of them. There is also a Preaching of Peter.

The Revelation of Peter was for a time considered authentic, but was later so thoroughly repudiated that only fragments and disarranged texts now survive.

It is concerned with "last things:" second coming, judgment, heaven, and hell. It was no doubt originally composed in Greek, but parts at least of Ethiopic and Arabic translations have survived.

In the fairly long surviving Greek fragment the redeemed are described as follows:

"Then the Lord says, 'Let us go to the mountain, let us pray.'" Then Peter tells how "we twelve disciples, as we were going away with him, asked him to show us some of our upright brothers who have left the world, so we could see in what form they are, and having encouraged ourselves could encourage our hearers." "While we were praying, there suddenly appeared two men standing in front of the Lord, at whom we were not able to look; for there came from their countenance a ray as if from the sun, and their clothes were a brightness man's eyes never saw, neither is mouth able to explain or heart to understand the glory with which they were clothed and the beauty of their countenance." A few lines are devoted to these specimens of the redeemed, and then heaven itself is described in language reminiscent of Lucian.

The rest of the fragment, about two pages, is taken up with a horribly repulsive description of the damned, who are pictured as receiving punishments specially suited to their crimes, and

113

apparently going far beyond eye for eye and tooth for tooth. Only a mind full of hate and sadistically morbid could get any satisfaction out of these pictures of hell. But perhaps they were valued as effective scarecrows, rather than because they were a delight to depraved minds.

Like the Greek of the other two Christian apocalypses, the language of this work is quite simple.

It has been assigned an early second century date because it is included in a late second century list, the Muratorian Canon, and is commented on by Clement of Alexandria as Scripture. Eusebius rejected it, but Sozomen, an early fifth century historian, says it was read for a long time in certain churches of Palestine.

CHAPTER V

Letters and Treatises

1. HEBREWS

This treatise interprets the nature and career of Jesus in a striking figure of speech, representing him as the infinitely powerful and effective high priest for all time, "a priest forever, after the order of Melchizedek," who once for all offered himself as the all-sufficient sacrifice, who then entered the holy of holies, heaven itself, and engages there in high-priestly prayer for his people.

The document opens with a sonorous period recalling in one majestic sweep all past ages of God's gracious revelations, and the culminating revelation through his son at the end of the ages.

The appropriateness of the address, "To the Hebrews," lies in its use of Hebrew temple worship as the basic feature of the book. The Hebrew religion is interpreted as a prophetic symbol of the actual religion of the future, which has been realized through the priestly office of Jesus.

The language of the book is impressive, a fitting vehicle for the exalted grandeur achieved in the combination of universal history and universal religion. Aside from the opening sentence, the best known flight of rhetoric is the "faith chapter," 9, with its array of martyrs past and present, who constitute for us both a spectacle to behold and a stadium full of spectators before whom we are to run our race, with our eyes fixed on the chief of martyrs.

The work was no doubt intended primarily for Christians, though Jews would find it more interesting than most Christian writings. At least they are in a better position to interpret its figures.

Its date is a puzzle. It represents an advanced stage in the attempts to explain the character and work of Jesus, but it is not in the tradition that eventually became standard, nor is it more advanced than the Fourth Gospel. Even our earliest Christian documents, Paul's letters, already explain Jesus as the earthly manifestation of a pre-existent divine being, the acting agent in the creation of the universe, who while incarnate made universal salvation possible by his sacrificial martyrdom, who returned to an even more commanding heavenly participation in the functions of deity, and who was to appear again in visible form to inaugurate the Messianic era. Hebrews seems to have been written late enough that the lively expectation of his early return had faded, probably toward the end of the first century.

Most systematic readers of the New Testament experience sooner or later a special enthusiasm for this book, amply justifying its place in the canon; but how any Greek reader could consider it the work of Paul is hard to see. Clement of Alexandria, the earliest extant writer to discuss the question, quoted by Eusebius in Church History 6.14.2-4, obviously recognizes the difference from Paul's Greek, and suggests that Hebrews was translated from Hebrew by Luke. Origen, quoted by Eusebius, Church History 6.25.11-14, indulges in similar speculations. Tertullian says, On Modesty 20, that it is ascribed to Barnabas. Translations into other languages have removed the linguistic evidence, so that most Christians have accepted Hebrews as the work of Paul. The *tour de force* of this ascription must have been perpetrated in the latter half of the second century to make possible its inclusion in the canon, apostolic authority being required before a book could be considered Scripture. With this book it was never a question of intrinsic merit. Marcion did not include it in his collection of Pauline letters, but the later traditional list of fourteen letters included

Hebrews and the three Pastorals. Conjecture as to the authorship of Hebrews is futile.

2. EPHESIANS

This document is an eloquent compendium of Pauline doctrine, devotion and ethics. The language has a peculiar beauty and distinction, though bordering on the florid. There is a pronounced richness in the carefully constructed archetectonic sentences. The whole epistle might be described in its own words, "a harmoniously constructed building" "standing as a holy temple" "on the foundation of the apostles and prophets," with "Jesus Christ himself as the chief corner stone."

It is written in the popular Greek of the time, but of a style comparable to the art and beauty of the Greek Orthodox liturgy, in which it is quite at home. It is a prose poem with grandly flowing sentences. A fine appreciation was composed by Philip Schaff in his *History of the Christian Church*, Vol. I, ad loc.

Ephesians is the source of a number of popular evangelical quotations, e.g., "the unsearchable riches of Christ," "the manifold wisdom of God," "the unity of the spirit in the bond of peace," "carried about by every wind of doctrine," "By grace you are saved through faith, and that not of yourselves, it is the gift of God," "one Lord, one faith, one baptism." The English of the last quotation is rather flat in comparison with the Greek, because in Greek each of the three nouns is a different gender, requiring a different word for "one."

A Pauline exhortation to upright living and personal piety, begun toward the end of the fourth chapter, continues to the end of the book, closing with the well-known figure of the moral panoply, which is borrowed from Isaiah.

AUTHORSHIP AND DATE

If one follows the conservative principle of making no change unless he is sure it ought to be made, he will leave Ephesians in its traditional place among Paul's letters; but the more scientific principle of being guided by probability, however slight, would place Ephesians among the later books of the New Testament. The problem is difficult. Leading scholars take opposite sides.

There seems to be very little in this epistle that might not have been written by Paul. The references to apostles and prophets, 2:30, 3:5, suggest the viewpoint of a later writer. Being built on the foundation of the apostles and prophets is a contradiction of First Corinthians 3:4, where Jesus Christ is the only foundation. Paul's letters however are by no means free from inconsistencies, as pointed out in the discussion of Galatians. There are a number of affinities with First Peter. Professor Antoniades notes thirteen in his Patriarchates' edition of the Greek Testament. Among these is the reference to the descent to Hades, 4:9. Compare with First Peter 3:19 and 4:6. Nowhere else does Paul use such an expression as "holy apostles," 3:5. The greatest affinities are found in Colossians. It has been suggested that the writer had Colossians before him when he wrote.

One of the strongest arguments against Pauline authorship is found in the impersonal tone of the epistle. The oldest manuscript of the opening page of Ephesians does not have the words "in Ephesus." There is no reference to Ephesus anywhere in the whole document. The writing lacks the everyday naturalness of Colossians and the undisputed Pauline letters. This naturalness is achieved partly by parentheses, anacoloutha, and the first and second persons. The treatise is of a general character, rather than in any way meeting a definite situation. This fact, combined with the others mentioned above, has given rise to the hypothesis that it was composed by an enthusiastic Paulinist to serve as an introduction to the Pauline corpus, though it is not clear just why anyone should want such an introduction. It seems more reasonable to suppose that some such summary was circulated before the corpus was formed, or that it was a digest of what letters the compiler had, after the manner of Tatian's Diatessaron, which was a continuous narrative put together from the materials of all four Gospels.

The second sentence of Ephesians, with its 202 words, corresponds in content to the third sentence of Colossians with its 268 words. The sentence in Ephesians is a highly elaborated blessing, involving a rhapsodic statement of catholic theology.

Each recognized Pauline letter, except Galatians, has a formal thanksgiving immediately following the formal greeting. Each of these thanksgivings, except in Second Corinthians, begins with "I thank God." Second Corinthians has "Blessed be God." Each of the thanksgivings is personal, telling how Paul thanks God for those to whom he is writing. Ephesians, like Second Corinthians, has a blessing instead of a thanksgiving, but unlike all such passages, it is impersonal. The application of this test results in one more count against the authenticity of Ephesians and the Pastorals.

Another test is the use of the words Satan and devil. As stated in connexion with Second Thessalonians, this test places Ephesians among the later books.

Still another test is the list of church officials, in which Ephesians resembles the earlier books, for it speaks, 4:11, of apostles, prophets, evangelists, pastors, and teachers, instead of bishops, priests (elders), and deacons. However, the terms evangelist and pastor are not found in the undisputed writings of Paul. Ephesians must have been written between 70 and 90.

The references to supernatural beings in 1:21, 2:2, and 6:12 were listed along with other Pauline usage in the discussion of Galatins, p. 39.

3. First Peter

We are now at the ragged border between the books that barely got into the New Testament and those that were finally excluded. First Peter belongs to the little group of seven known as the Catholic Epistles, viz., James, First and Second Peter, First, Second, and Third John, Jude. First Peter is perhaps the earliest of the seven.

The general impression given by First Peter is Pauline ideas presented with a certain elegance and polish of language. Some of the sayings have become proverbial, such as, "the devil goes about like a roaring lion, seeking whom he may devour," "heirs of the grace of life," "like newborn babes desiring the sincere milk of the word," "things the prophets desired to look into," "If the righteous scarcely are saved, where shall the ungodly and sinners appear?"

It has been suggested that First Peter is our earliest example of the Roman Church speaking in Peter's name. It imitates some of the more obvious features of Paul's letters. Judging from the language, it was not written by Clement.

Features in harmony with usage at the turn of the century are: the figure of the stone building, developed by Hermas in Vision 3 to a tiresome length; and the appropriation of the Jewish heritage, even exclusion of Jews, so that the real "kingdom of priests," Exodus 19: 6, First Peter 2: 9, is now the Church instead of Israel, reminiscent of Clement's use of the Aaronic and Levitical priesthoods as models of church order.

Due partly to such pronouncements of brotherhood and equality as Paul had made to the Galatians, there was in early Christianity a natural tendency for slaves to assert their rights. This seems to have caused some embarrassment to Christian leaders, who resorted to the subterfuge, still flourishing in some quarters, that the equality and brotherhood are spiritual, not literal or physical. Paul had to tell the slaves at Corinth not to try to gain their freedom. Christ was coming soon anyhow. First Peter has a more impressive repression of abolitionist views, though the consolation of Christ's speedy return is lacking—another indication of late date.

The exhortation to slaves is followed by a fling at women's dress, that has served as an excuse for much modern ranting among Protestants and for specific taboos in the Roman Church.

The affinities of language are rather with Ephesians and other books near the turn of the century. At the beginning and end of First Peter there is obvious imitation of Pauline epistolary forms, i.e., salutation, thanksgiving, and close. Pauline ideas occur with only less frequency than in Ephesians. There are telltale items indicating a post-Petrine date. One of these is devil instead of Satan. Peter would have been less likely than Paul to use the Greek word devil. Babylon for Rome is, in the New Testament, shared only with Revelation. There are five parallels with Clement of Rome, one with the Shepherd, and one with Ignatius' letter to the Ephesians. There is also the use of presbyter (priest) for pastor. The earliest *haustafel* (summary of mutual obligations within a household) in early Chris-

120

tian literature is in Colossians. It is probably the source of those in the Pastorals, Ephesians, and First Peter.

Of the dozen or so apparent affinities with Ephesians, one is 3:18-20, about Christ preaching to the spirits in prison, which seems to agree with Ephesians 4:8-10. In spite of Rendel Harris' interesting conjecture that First Peter here refers to Enoch, whose name was then lost by a copyist's error, it seems that Christ fits the context better than Enoch.

One should freely admit that there are question-begging elements in all appeals to Revelation, Ephesians, and the Pastorals. However, this appeal will work in reverse. No book of undisputed early date uses "devil," or "presbyter," or Babylon.

It seems certain that Peter was crucified at Rome under Nero, as explained above, p. 59f. The strongest argument against Petrine authorship of First Peter is the unlikelihood of Peter being able to write such Greek. No doubt he had picked up some colloquial Greek here and there, but it is unlikely that he could write it, especially the kind found here, which is of higher literary level than that of a native speaker like Paul. The ancient Church assumed that Peter needed an interpreter when preaching at Rome, i.e., to a Greek-speaking audience. But Sylvanus is said in the closing words to be the one through whom Peter writes, and so the Greek might be his. More likely he is the messenger who is supposed to have carried the letter.

The second century tradition that Mark was Peter's interpreter may have been taken from the closing words of First Peter. Elsewhere in the New Testament Mark, member of a Cypriote family, is associated either with his relative Barnabas, or with Paul. This use of names of two of Paul's companions, Sylvanus and Mark, is one of the apparent borrowings from Paul's letters. It has been remarked that to find companions for apostles, it seems to have been necessary to go to Paul's letters.

The place of writing is given as Babylon, a pseudonym for Rome, as clearly shown in Revelation. No doubt this is an imitation, if not an actual borrowing from Hebrew usage, still in vogue in the twentieth century, in which some nations are referred to by Old Testament names. A similar, if not related, practice is the use of names of extinct dioceses to designate some modern bishops.

Under Nero there was apparently no persecution in Asia Minor. Whether the trouble under Domitian was more widespread than Revelation indicates is not certain. As far as the references in First Peter go, they might well refer to the persecution with which Pliny the Younger helped in the days of Trajan. The exhortation to civil loyalty is in sharp contrast to the bitter hatred expressed in Revelation.

4. First Clement

Clement, bishop of Rome near the end of Domitian's reign, wrote this letter to the church at Corinth. It was included in some ancient copies of the New Testament. It is the earliest of the Apostolic Fathers and contains our earliest testimony to the martyrdoms of Paul and Peter, but the testimony is given with the tantalizing indefiniteness that characterizes so many primary sources.

The general purpose of the letter is to restore peace and order after a rebellion in the church at Corinth. Several of the Apostolic Fathers, as well as some books of the New Testament, testify to the struggles and disorders that accompanied the evolution of the Christian hierarchy.

In chapters 42 and 44 Clement gives a form of the doctrine of the apostolic succession: God sent out Jesus Christ, the Lord Jesus Christ sent the apostles, the apostles appointed bishops and deacons. The point was, of course, that the Christians at Corinth should obey the officials who stood in this authentic succession. It was a device to secure unity in the Church. The same argument is presented for the same purpose in the Fourth Gospel: "Just as the Father sent me, so I am sending you," John 20:21.

In the same connexion Clement offers the sociologically and psychologically sound argument that the Hebrews had a similar succession of religious leaders, viz., God had appointed Moses, Moses had established the offices of priests and Levites, and these had come down in regular succession. The appeal to Hebrew models for Christian institutions was a common form of argument in the early Church.

Clement clearly states that his letter is not only for the benefit of the Corinthians, but for the Romans as well, i.e., he hopes it, like Paul's letters, will be read in other churches. Clement however falls far short of Paul in vigor and pointedness. Much of his letter is labored and tiresome.

A passage of curious interest is chapter 25, where Clement reports the legend of the Phoenix, the unique African bird that lived five hundred years. As the time of its death approached it made a nest of frankincense, myrrh, and other spices. In this nest it died, and a worm was produced in its decaying body. This worm developed into the new Phoenix, which took the nest and bones of its predecessor to Egypt and deposited them there on the altar of the sun in Heliopolis. This passage is perhaps the one feature that would in our judgment bar First Clement from the New Testament. To the ancient reader the fatal defect was no doubt the certainty of its post-apostolic date.

In one place the letter is reminiscent of Hebrews. This long passage on Old Testament worthies may be a reworking of "the faith chapter," but the subject was likely a common rhetorical theme in the Church of that day. It has also been suggested that in his letter Clement is making an effort to carry out the exhortation of Hebrews 5:11 f. to assume his teaching function.

His Greek is a plain, sober, simple Koiné; a contrast to the wordy colloquialism of his garrulous contemporary, Hermas; a contrast befitting the dignity of the bishop, as against the undisciplined talk of a former slave and would-be occupant of the front seat.

Clement quotes the Septuagint frequently and at length. His style and thought are prosaic, except for the prayers, perhaps quoted, which rise to the impressive force and dignity of the Greek Orthodox liturgy.

5. THE PASTORALS

FIRST AND SECOND TIMOTHY AND TITUS

By this time the Church had formed some definite ideas as to what sort of man a pastor should be, no doubt learning largely from horrible examples of what one should not be. Men like

Hermas, who could not rule their own families, wanted to rule congregations; others regarded it as a pastor's privilege to liberally gladden his heart with wine; there had been disgraceful examples of lazy, careless, unfriendly, dishonest, ignorant, quarrelsome, stubborn, greedy, grasping, sacrilegious presbyters; there had even been bigamists in holy orders. Besides, some new, very green converts had felt called to start preaching right away, and had made contributions of doubtful value. Moreover, some of the clergy had wives who were misfits as pastors' helpmeets; so the writer of these epistles prepared three quite useful tracts, stating simply, and in terms not easily forgotten, just what was and is expected of the clergy, both in public and private.

Christians had already given up the hope that every church member would be an ornament to his profession, but were at least demanding that their leaders be above reproach. Thus the Pastoral Epistles put the official stamp on the double standard.

Not only morals, but also doctrine was giving administrators considerable concern. The second century witnessed as critical a struggle with Docetism and Gnosticism as the first century had with Judaizing, so time and time again the Pastorals exhort ministers to be orthodox. It has always been a problem in Christendom as to how fully and literally the Old Testament should be accepted. The middle of the second century saw the extreme reaction against the Jewish Bible. The advocacy of celibacy was also on the increase. So the Pastorals assert that all of the Scriptures, i.e., the Old Testament, are divinely inspired. They also offer a corrective to Paul's monastic statements in First Corinthians.

These three epistles, First and Second Timothy and Titus, have met the test of classics. They offer instruction and advice which is still useful to those preparing for the Christian ministry. Ordination and installation sermons are still based on texts found in them.

The Pastorals bear the name of Paul, but whether he had anything to do with their writing is a puzzling problem. Some think we have here a case of expansion like the thirteen Ignatian letters expanded from seven shorter ones. Attempts have been made to pick out original passages by the hand of Paul, but the results have not won general acceptance.

It seems plain enough that there are post-Pauline elements in these treatises, e.g., our old friends "devil" and "presbyter," as well as "bishop." The last term is found in Philippians, but nowhere else in undisputed early books. The typical Pauline list of primitive leaders is missing from the Pastorals, i.e., apostles, prophets, and teachers. That the early Church did not regard the Pastorals as the work of Paul is almost certainly proven by their absence from Marcion's Bible. That no one was deceived when they were published seems equally probable.

The literary parallels to features of these books make an impressive array. As far back as Sophocles, fifth century B.C., Antigone 661f., we find Greeks taking management of one's own household as a measure of capacity for larger responsibilities, though in the same play, 726, king Creon "despises" a man for his "youth." The Pastorals have eight parallels to Pauline letters, two each to Hebrews, the Shepherd, and the Didaché, four to Barnabas, six to Ignatius, three to Athenagoras, one each to First Clement, Tatian, Acts, and John; but most striking of all, eleven to Polycarp's letter to the Philippians, which appears to have been written between 110 and 120.

Upon examination of the numerous verbatim correspondences with Polycarp, it seems possible to regard them as clichés used independently by each writer. Some of the common phrases and clauses are: "Christ our hope," "that your progress may be manifest to all," "having loved this present age," "lest perchance God grant them repentance."

If a conjecture must be hazarded as to the date of the Pastorals, let it be the first quarter of the second century.

Writing in the third quarter of the second century, Theophilus of Antioch, in Autolycus 3.14, quotes First Timothy 2:2 as Scripture. Not much later Irenaeus, in Against Heresies 3.3.4, 12.11, ascribes both canonicity and Pauline authorship to the Pastorals.

It is particularly in the last chapter of Second Timothy that one is tempted to see a genuine Pauline fragment in the extended personal references. On this passage is founded the view that Paul was acquitted at his first trial at Rome, and was released.

Household regulations are somewhat expanded in the Pastorals. Both male and female slaves seem to have made the natural mistake of taking pronouncements of liberty, equality, and fraternity at their face value; so, as in Ephesians, their enthusiasm is curbed in no uncertain terms. "Let all who are slaves under the yoke yield all honor to their own worthy masters," First Timothy 6:1. "Let slaves be in every way subject to their own masters," Titus 2:9.

The warning in First Timothy 4:7 about pagan myths told by old women (old men should have been included) is still in point. Christendom is still saturated with pagan mythology. Some ancient mythological characters have been given new names, some not, as in the case of the three Fates and Charon.

The Pastorals contain significant evidence on organizational development. Regulations are given for admission to the order of widows. Young women are strictly forbidden. The references to presbyter and bishop were mentioned above.

An early Christian hymn is quoted in First Timothy 3:16:

> *Seen in the flesh,*
> *Justified in the spirit,*
> *Revealed to angels,*
> *Proclaimed to heathen,*
> *Believed on in the world,*
> *Received in glory.*

The Pastorals have furnished a number of well-known quotations, e.g., "Love of money is a root of all evils," First Timothy 6:10; "We brought nothing into the world, and can take nothing out of it," I Tim. 6:7; "For I know him in whom I have believed, and am persuaded that he is able to protect what I have entrusted to him until that day," II Tim. 1:12; "The word of God is not bound," II Tim. 2:9; "Study to show yourself acceptable, a workman who does not have to be ashamed, dividing the word of truth correctly," II Tim. 2:15; "Every Scripture is divinely inspired, and is profitable for instruction," etc., II Tim. 3:16; "Waging the good contest of the faith," I Tim. 6:12; and the words that sound like Paul's epitaph, "I have contended in the great game, I have finished the race, I have kept the faith; now there is reserved for me a wreath of uprightness, that the Lord, the just judge, will award me on that day," II Tim. 4:7-8.

Now and then the Greek resembles the Orthodox liturgy, which, with all its beauties, has nothing finer than "the blessed and only potentate, king of kings and Lord of lords, who alone has immortality, inhabiting unapproachable light, whom no man has seen or can see, to him be the honor and the eternal power! Amen." I Tim. 6:15.

6. Letters of Ignatius

Ignatius is the most spirited of the Apostolic Fathers, his emotional tension becoming morbid in some passages. This could be the work of an admirer exaggerating his hero's reaction to impending martyrdom.

In the reign of Trajan, Ignatius, bishop of Antioch in Syria, was condemned to die at Rome. So says Eusebius, Church History 3.36. On his way to Rome Ignatius wrote a letter to each of six churches and to one individual. The churches were Ephesus, Magnesia, Tralles, Rome, Philadelphia, and Smyrna; the individual was Polycarp, bishop of Smyrna. In Ephesians 12 Ignatius says he regards himself as an imitator of Paul. It has been suggested that he wrote to six churches because that was the number of churches addressed in the Pauline corpus of his day.

The bishop of Ephesus when Ignatius wrote was Onesimus. John Knox[1] argues convincingly that this was the same Onesimus about whom Paul wrote to Philemon, Apphia, Archippus, and the church that was in his house. Damas was bishop of Magnesia and Polybius of Tralles, but we are not told who were the bishops of Rome and Philadelphia. The letters are a mine of testimony to several phases of developing Christianity.

There is important evidence on the dates of writing and

---

[1] *Philemon among the Letters of Paul,* Chicago 1936.

canonization of New Testament books. It is assumed that Ignatius, like Marcion, did not recognize the Pastorals; but he has numerous parallels to them. These parallels may be exhibited as follows:

Ignatius	New Test.	Ignatius	New Test.
Eph 14.1	1 Tm 1:4-5	Rm 7.3	2 Tm 2:8
Eph 18.2	2 Tm 2:8	Sm 10.2	2 Tm 1:16
Mg 6.2	Tit 2:7	Phl 1.3	2 Tm 4:1
Mg 8.1	I Tm 1:3-4	Pol. 6.2	2 Tm 2:4
	Tit 1:14, 3:9		

There are several Synoptic parallels, mostly to Matthew, viz., "If the prayer of two or three has such power," "Those who are not of the father's planting," "The pleasures of the world will profit me nothing," "the tree is manifest by its fruits," "the Lord received the perfume on his head," "a star in the sky outshone all other stars," "that he might fulfill all righteousness," "he bore our diseases," "be wise as a serpent in all things, and harmless as a dove." There is a close parallel to Luke 24: 39-42 in Smyrneans 3.2-3, stating that the risen Lord invited his disciples to touch him and see that he was not a disembodied spirit, and that he ate and drank like a fleshly being. There seems to be a reference in Magnesians 5.1 to Acts 1:25, where Judas is said to have "gone to his own place." There are at least two parallels to the Fourth Gospel, viz., Philadelphians 7.1 and John 8:14, "He knew where he came from and where he is going;" and Magnesians 8.2, John 8:29, "who in all things pleased the one who sent him."

Ignatius mentions no Gospel by name, yet the Gospels and epistles are so close to canonization that much doubt can be cast on the theory that Marcion was the first to regard any of our New Testament as Scripture. The following passages show that for Ignatius the "gospel" was canonical: "fleeing to the gospel as to the flesh of Jesus," Philadelphians 5.1; "We love the prophets because they announce the gospel," Ph. 5.2; "whom the prophets have not persuaded, nor the Law of Moses, nor even to this day the gospel," Smyrneans 5.1; "Attend to the prophets, but especially to the gospel," Sm. 7.2.

In the history of doctrine special interest attaches to Ignatius' attacks on Docetism, e.g., "So be dumb when they speak to you apart from Jesus Christ, who is of the family of David, who is from Mary, who was really born, who ate and drank, who was really persecuted under Pontius Pilate, who was really crucified and died, while those of heaven, earth, and the lower world were watching, who also really rose from the dead," Trallians 9.1-2. A form of the last clause became crystallized in the customary Eastern Orthodox Easter greeting.

In condemnation of Jewish custom he has the following to say: "No longer sabbatizing, but living according to the Lord's Day," Magnesians 9.1; "It is inconsistent to talk about Jesus Christ and to Judaize," Mg. 10.3; "If anyone expounds Judaism to you, don't listen to him. For it is better to hear Christianity from a circumcised man than Judaism from the uncircumcised," Philadelphians 6.1.

It is hardly necessary to mention the complete deification of Jesus attested by Ignatius, for that process was virtually complete in Paul's day, or at least in the letters that are ascribed to him. In both Paul and Ignatius some think they see the hand of a later writer or editor. Some statements must be recognized as Binitarian, rather than Trinitarian. Except in the benediction at the close of Second Corinthians, Paul does not refer to a distinct person that can be properly translated "the Holy Spirit." Such figurative language as that of Ephesians 9.1 indicates something less than personification, though literally Ignatius writes "the holy spirit." It seems certain that in some early writers, e.g., Hermas, the phrase "holy spirit" without the article, should be rendered "a spirit of holiness." Perhaps the correct translation in Ignatius, Eph. 9.1 is "the spirit of holiness." It is probably anachronistic to read personification and the doctrine of the Trinity into Paul and Ignatius, let alone Hermas.

The most persistent note in the Ignatian letters is insistence on full loyalty to the three traditional orders of the clergy, viz., bishop, priest (presbyter), and deacon. Here a definite development has occurred since Paul's time. One gets the impression that the presbyters were still assistant pastors, though there is nothing inconsistent with the view that individual presbyters were assigned to conduct services in outlying chapels, while the bishop presided in the mother church of any given city. Deacons seem to have been assistants attached more closely to the bishop, and among other things, to have had the function of messengers to distant churches. The chief reason for insistence on obedience to the clergy seems to have been the anxiety of Ignatius for unity, to which he refers several times: Ephesians 4.1-2; 5; 6; 13.2; Magnesians 1.2.

In the last paragraph of the letter to Smyrna "the virgins who are called widows" are referred to. This should be compared with instructions concerning the order of widows in First Timothy 5.1-16, and with Paul's remarks on celibacy in First Corinthians 7:7, 25-28. There is no doubt that monasticism and celibacy developed early in Christianity.

It is clear from Ignatius' letter to Polycarp, 5.2, that it took the Church some time to establish the practice of sanctifying marriage with a Christian ceremony, at least among gentiles.

One of the oftenest quoted passages from Ignatius is Smyrneans 8.2, where the phrase "the catholic church" appears for the first time in extant writings. The correct translation of the sentence seems to be, "Wherever Jesus Christ is, there is the universal church," or better, "The whole church is conterminous with the body of Christ, just as a real congregation is always found in the presence of a bishop."

Sacramentalism is far developed along the lines of the Pauline-Johannine, or Ephesian tradition. An altar is regularly spoken of, and transubstantiation certainly implied, e.g., Smyrneans 7.1, "because they do not acknowledge that the eucharist is the flesh of our Savior Jesus Christ."

Notable figurative interpretations are: "faith is the Lord's flesh and love is his blood," "the bishop is God the father, and the deacon is the commandment of God," "the eucharist is the medicine of immortality."

Ethics has already become Christianity's buried talent, barely mentioned in a few places.

His own impending martyrdom is the almost exclusive theme

of the letter to the Romans. He fears their love will injure him. It will be hard for him to "achieve God" if they fail to spare him. He is afraid they will secure his pardon. He thinks he will be worth more to the Church as a dead martyr than as a live bishop, since he will have demonstrated that he is a Christian in fact, not merely in word. He beseeches the Roman church to stand aside and let him go as food to the carnivores, for he is God's wheat to be ground to fine flour by their teeth. He prays the bodies of the animals may become his grave, so that after his death he may be a burden to no one. He will entice the wild beasts to devour him. If they are unwilling he will provoke them. He gloats over the thought of fire and cross, of being torn limb from limb, of having his bones scattered and his limbs crushed. "Let the evil torments of the devil come on me, only let me achieve Christ!" "Let none of you aid the ruler of this world by depriving me of the joy of martyrdom!" How different all this ranting from, "Abba, father, all things are possible to you! Take this cup away from me!"

So popular were the letters of Ignatius that some later admirer expanded the seven to make thirteen. In Latin the Ignatian letter collection finally grew to fifteen, and in the west the revision superseded the shorter list. It was not till the beginning of modern historical criticism that the expansion was detected. Archbishop Ussher, though best known for his dating of creation, should on the other hand be given credit for his acumen concerning the Ignatian letters. The definitive work on the problem is Bishop Lightfoot's.

There is some incoherence in the letter to Polycarp, where the writer sometimes seems to forget he is writing to the bishop himself, and tells the people to pay attention to the bishop. Does he imagine himself in church in presence of both parties?

Polycarp, in his letter to the Philippians, says he is sending the letters of Ignatius they have ordered, including the one Ignatius had written to him as well as the others he had. It was perhaps the existence of the Pauline letter collection that so quickly moved these two parties to acquire an Ignatian collection. It is noteworthy that both the Pauline and Ignatian later suffered accretion.

First John, with its brief companion pieces, gives us a strongly marked sampling of the Ephesian spirit. The similarity to the air of the Fourth Gospel is unmistakable. If the four documents are not by the same author, they are at least by kindred souls. The warmth of Paul and Ignatius is in them all. Of great simplicity and emotional power, they make an indelible impression by the effective repetition of a few themes. No wonder the Gospel and letters became so popular.

First John rings the changes on light, truth, and love. "God is love." "We love him because he first loved us." "We show that we love him if we keep his commandments." "His commandment is that we love one another." "Anyone who does not love his brother whom he has seen, cannot love God whom he has not seen."

Anti-Docetism is one of the express motives of this letter. "This is the one who came by water and blood, not by water alone, but by water and by blood." A century later Cyprian reprimands those in his diocese who were using water alone in their communion service. Perhaps Mithraism as well as Docetism was involved.

At this same point in First John was added, first in the Latin, the famous textual corruption of 5:7 on the Trinity.

In 5:16 a distinction is made between a deadly sin and a sin not deadly. In various forms this distinction is found in several documents of the period.

Second John is addressed by the presbyter to the elect lady, and to her children. It seems the lady is a church and the children are the members. The closing sentence supports this interpretation: "The children of your elect sister salute you."

The general theme is the same as that of First John: Love one another, which is keeping God's commandments; avoid the Docetist, who is the anti-Christ, because he does not confess that Jesus Christ came in the flesh.

Instead of writing more, he plans to come and see them.

Third John is addressed by the presbyter to the beloved

Gaius. He has no greater joy than to hear that his children are walking in the truth. He praises Gaius for his hospitality. He has written to the church, but Diotrephes, who likes to have charge of affairs, would not accept him, has not been hospitable himself, and will not permit others to be. The presbyter will reprove him when he comes. He has heard good reports of Demetrius. He is not writing more because he hopes to come immediately.

The three Johannine letters are not mentioned in any extant literature before the end of the second century, but Eusebius, Church History 3.39.17, says that Papias quoted First John. It was therefore known by the third decade of the second century. The other two letters are probably contemporary.

Conjecture as to the authorship of these letters is futile. It is quite possible the second and third are not by the same author as the first. It is reasonably sure they are not by John the son of Zebedee.

8. JAMES

When James is translated into present day English, it is quite effective. The archaisms of translations made centuries ago are particularly objectionable in this work.

Most of us feel our conscience stirred by the pointed observations of this moralist. We know what a damaging blow we give our religious profession when we fail to control our tongue, and we clearly recognize the truth that a religious conviction that does not affect behavior is a dead and worthless delusion. How like certain passages in Amos, Hosea, Micah, and Isaiah is the reminder that "a type of ritual that is pleasing to our God and father is to look after orphans and widows that are in trouble." This insistence on ethical expression of religion suggests an early date for James, for Christianity soon permitted first things to come last. It is good to be told we must blame our sins on ourselves, instead of on God or the devil.

James agrees with later books of the New Testament in using the word devil, but reference to the Christian meeting as a synagogue suggests a date not later than the first quarter of the second century. It was no doubt anti-Jewish feeling that put an end to this usage as well as to Sabbatarianism.

The book clearly reflects persecution, both at the beginning and elsewhere. Wavering souls with a tendency to lapse under pressure are roundly denounced. People of wealth already belonged to the Church, for the writer condemns undue deference paid to them. Paul's writings are known, and reflection on them has made clear the danger of understanding *faith* to mean *belief,* and in this sense the sole requisite for salvation. However, the writer does not seem to realize that Paul's glowing faith was much more than intellectual conviction, but rather a powerful emotion finding inevitable expression in good deeds.

From the above considerations we may conjecture that James was written shortly after the persecution under Domitian, possibly a little later, after the one under Trajan.

James has had an influence out of proportion to its size. A number of passages have become proverbial, and it has furnished the scriptural basis for two of the seven sacraments, viz., anointing and penance. "Is one of you sick? Let him call the presbyters of the church, and let them pray over him after anointing him with oil in the name of the Lord; and the prayer of faith will save the sufferer; and the Lord will get him up," 5: 14-15. The Roman Church has specialized this sacrament into extreme unction. It is also a sacrament in the Orthodox Church, but not limited to the dying. The warrant for penance is found in 5: 16, "Confess your sins to one another that you may be healed, for a good man's urgent prayer is very powerful."

James is first mentioned by Origen, in the third century. Eusebius, in Church History 2.23, regards it as pseudonymous, classing it among the disputed books, though most churches were using it as Scripture.

The ascription to James is no doubt a mere literary device, loosely attached to the text, and at the time of writing deceiving no one. If the suggested date is correct, it could not have been any of the Jameses named among the Twelve, nor is it likely that any of them wrote Greek.

9. JUDE

Jude is a bitter little tract against heresy, full of Old Testament illustrations, and with an interest in apocalyptic legend. The writer regarded the Assumption of Moses and the Apocalypse of Enoch as Scripture, as shown in 9 f. and 14 f. He refers to the Lord Jesus Christ in a way to indicate he has no intention of palming off his work as an apostolic document. The title is only a pen name. Jude, Judas, and Judah are all the same name, though this fact is easily overlooked.

The closing sentence of the tract makes an excellent liturgical piece. The Greek of the main text is of a somewhat literary type, though the writer regards Paul as his model.

Jude is not mentioned by name before the end of the second century, but was used by Second Peter. It was one of the very latest writings to find acceptance as part of the New Testament.

10. PAPIAS

The writings of this Apostolic Father have perished, except for fragments quoted by later writers. Bishop of Hierapolis in Asia in the reign of Hadrian and/or Antoninus Pius. Eusebius, Church History 3.39.13, says he was a man of "very little sense," probably basing his judgment on the extravagant millennialism of Papias.

The chief interest in Papias concerns what he has to say about the three Gospels, Mark, Matthew, and John. In Church History 3.9 Eusebius quotes a passage in which Papias says he was a hearer of John and a companion of Polycarp. The passage seems to mean that Papias associated with the presbyters of his day to learn the words of the apostles Andrew, Peter, Philip, Thomas, James, John, and Matthew, things that Aristion and the presbyter John had to tell, for Papias said he would rather learn from the "living and abiding voice," than get his information out of books.

Following the example of Eusebius, later scholars have made endless attempts to get at the meaning of Papias. His statements about our First and Second Gospels are reported in connexion with these Gospels. Irenaeus used Papias in a desperate attempt to prove the Fourth Gospel was written by the son of Zebedee. He too has had many followers.

Other Papias fragments report legends about Judas Iscariot, the fallen angels, views on the authenticity of Revelation, the martyrdom of John at the hand of Jews in fulfillment of Jesus' prophecy that he and James would indeed drink the cup he was going to. It is from Papias that the idea of two Johns at Ephesus is derived.

Papias wrote the first known introduction to the study of the New Testament, entitled "Interpretation of the Lord's Oracles." This seems to have been written shortly before the middle of the second century.

11. SECOND PETER

This is apparently the latest book in the New Testament. The most striking proof of lateness is the definite recognition of Paul's letters as Scripture. As stated in the section on Ignatius, we do not have to credit Marcion with the canonization of Paul's letters. It would doubtless have occurred without Marcion, and perhaps did. It is therefore not necessary to date Second Peter after Marcion. Second Peter may be our earliest witness to the canonization. All we know about the date of Second Peter is that he freely quotes about one fourth of Jude. It would seem reasonable to date it in the second quarter of the second century, contemporary with Papias. It shows traces of Clement of Rome and of Hermas. In the latter half of the second century it was quoted by Theophilus of Antioch, *To Autolycus* 2.9, who probably regarded it as Scripture. The Greek shows the increasing tendency of second century writers to use literary language, though the writer also imitates the formalities of letter writing established by Paul and followed in First Peter.

The writer, being a far less bitter contender for the faith than the author of Jude, apparently felt that when he did have to denounce heresy, he could do no better than borrow the language of Jude. This tract had a most difficult time getting a foothold in the New Testament. Even Jerome was willing to suspect its canonicity. It is the New Testament's most certain example of publication under an assumed name.

Conclusion

No field of history, probably, has been investigated more thoroughly, or by a greater number, or by more competent scholars, than that of early Christianity. Many of these scholars however, have not enjoyed freedom of expression, or even of thought. Those who have felt free have usually agreed on certain major results regarding authors, dates, and accuracy of the various New Testament books. Discrepancies have been pointed out which anyone might have seen for himself, but few of us did. Traditional views have sometimes been confirmed, sometimes proven wrong.

There is not a book in the New Testament that is not attributed to an apostle or to a close friend of an apostle. For about half of the books these traditions seem mistaken. Perhaps the most revolutionary of all the general agreements of modern historians is that no New Testament book, as it now stands, was written by a personal friend of Jesus, i.e., by an eyewitness of his ministry. A few seem not to have been written before the year 120.

Along with these negative results, the historicity of Jesus has been firmly established, so there are few if any who now suggest that such a person as Jesus never lived.

Many who have fully accepted the results of modern historical study still regard the New Testament as a treasure house of inspiration and idealism. There are others who manage to hold modern historical views and traditional theological beliefs at the same time.

There have been attempts to produce expurgated editions of the New Testament by removing all elements offensive to modern intellectual taste. Such highly sterilized productions have proven less attractive, less interesting, than the complete documents in their ancient form; and are generally insipid, adding nothing to compensate for the interest of what has been removed.

Whatever the effect on organized religion, and on choices for devotional reading, the frank acceptance of the findings of historical study can, in the long run, be only for the common good.

APPENDIX I

Historical Chart

CIVIL AUTHORITIES	RELIGIOUS LEADERS	LITERARY EVENTS
Alexander the Great born 356 B.C. Battle of Issus 333 B.C. Seleucid era began 312 B.C.		
		Translation of the LXX begins in 3rd century B.C.
Antiochus Epiphanes reigned 175-164 B.C. Judah Maccabee rededicated the Temple 165 B.C. Pompey annexed Palestine to Roman Empire c. 65 B.C. Julius Caesar assassinated 44 B.C. Cicero murdered 43 B.C.		Wisdom of Sirach (Ecclesiasticus), beginning of Enoch literature, Book of Enoch, Book of Daniel LXX completed in first century B.C. Lucretius 1st half of 1st century B.C. Vergil last half of 1st Century B.C.
Augustus emperor 31 B.C.—14 A.D. Tiberius emperor 14-37 Caligula emperor 37-41 Claudius emperor 41-54 Nero emperor 54-68	Hillel 70 B.C.- 6 A.D. Jesus b. 8-4 B.C. crucified 27-30 Paul converted c. 30, at Corinth 50-52	Livy 59 B.C.-7 A.D.

I Thessalonians c. 50 Paul's letters written 49-64 |
| | Paul executed at Rome c. 65 Peter crucified at Rome c. 65 | |
| Galba, Otho, and Vitellius 68-69 Vespasian emperor 69-79 Titus emperor 79-81 | | Gospel of Mark c. 70 Gospel of Matthew c. 80 Luke-Acts 80-90 |

CIVIL AUTHORITIES	RELIGIOUS LEADERS	LITERARY EVENTS
Domitian emperor 81-96	Clement bishop at Rome	
Nerva emperor 96-98		I Clement c. 96, Revelation
Trajan emperor 98-117	Epictetus	Shepherd of Hermas, Suetonius, Didache
Hadrian emperor 117-138	Ignatius Papias	Pastorals, Gospel of John Johannine Letters, Ignatian Letters, Tacitus, Annals Plutarch 48-120
Antoninus Pius emperor 138-161		Letter of Polycarp, Martyrdom of Polycarp Diatessaron
	Polycarp 69 (?)-155	Apology & Dialog with Trypho
Marcus Aurelius emperor 161-180	Tatian Marcion	Lucian floruit, 160
Commodus emperor 180-192	Justin Martyr died c. 166	Theophilus of Antioch To Autolycus c. 182
Pertinax, Didius Julianus, Niger emperors 193	Tertullian b. 169 Irenaeus c.130-c.202 Clement of Alexandria 150?-215?	Against Heresies 180-200
Septimius Severus emperor 193-211	Origen 185?-254?	
Decius emperor 249-251	Cyprian d. 258	
Constantine emperor 306-337	Eusebius d. c. 340	Church Hist. (H. E.) c. 325

APPENDIX II

Passages Illustrative of Naive Concepts, etc.

When they saw him walking on the lake they thought it was a ghost. Mark 6:49, cf. Matthew 14:26.

They said, "You are raving." But she insisted it was so. And they said, "It is his angel." Acts 12:15.

He saw the sky being split. Mk 1:10-11. Cf. Mt 3:16, Lk 3:21-22, Acts 7:56, 10:11-16, Rev. 4:1.

From the end of the earth to the end of the sky. Mk. 13:27

Sky and earth will pass away. Mt. 24:35.

The sky was closed for three years and six months. Lk. 4:25.

He was carried up into the sky. Lk. 24:51.

He gave them bread from heaven (the sky) to eat. Jn. 6:31-58.

A voice came from heaven (the sky). Jn. 12:28.

As you saw him going (into the sky) so will he come again. Acts 1:10-11.

A sudden sound from heaven (the sky). Acts 2:2.

Jerusalem coming down from heaven, from God. Rev. 3:12.

The stars of the sky fell on the earth. Rev. 6:13.

The sky will be rolled up. Rev. 6:14.

Authority to close the sky. Rev. 11:6.

His tail pulls one-third of the stars of the sky. Rev. 12:4.

The angel of the Lord came down from heaven. Mt. 28:2.

The Lord's angel appeared to them. Lk. 2:9.

A multitude of the heavenly army. Lk. 2:13.

I saw Satan fallen from heaven (the sky). Lk. 10:18.

No one has gone back into heaven except the one who came down. Jn. 3:13.

I saw another mighty angel coming down from heaven (the sky).
Rev. 10:1.

Angels ministered to him. Mk. 1:13.

He will send the angels. Mk. 13:27.

An angel came down occasionally. Jn. 5:4.
(This verse not in the better manuscripts.)

Capernaum exalted to heaven (sky), put down to Hades. Mt. 11:23,
Lk 10:15.

In Hades lifting up his eyes. Lk. 16:23.

The gates of Hades will not prevail. Mt. 16:18.

Neither was he abandoned in Hades. Acts 2:31.

When the demon had been put out the mute spoke. Mt. 9:33.

He put out many demons. Mk. 1:34.

He met a man who had demons. Lk. 8:27.

Did this man sin, or his parents, that he was born blind? Jn. 9:2.

He will be filled with the Holy Spirit even before he is born. Lk. 1:15.

The babe leapt in my womb (because inspired by the Holy Spirit).
Lk. 1:41.

Their angels are always watching the face of my father in heaven.
Mt. 18:10.

Your names are inscribed in heaven. Lk. 10:20.

The Spirit coming down in bodily form like a dove. Lk. 3:22.

Who is at God's right hand, having gone into heaven. 1 Peter 3:22.

God is a spirit, and those who worship him must worship in spirit
and in truth. Jn. 4:24.

Inhabiting unapproachable light, whom no human being has seen
or can see. I Tim. 6:16.

APPENDIX III

The Sayings on the Cross

Eloi, Eloi, lama sabachthani. Mk. 15:34, Mt. 27:46.
(My God, my God, why have you abandoned me?)
    (Quotation from Ps. 22.)
Forgive them, Father, for they don't know what they are doing.
    Lk. 23:34.
    (Apparently not originally part of the Gospel. Source unknown.)
You will be with me today in paradise. Lk. 23:43.
Father, I entrust my spirit to your hands. Lk. 23:46.
    (Quotation from Ps. 31:5; part of Jewish children's bedtime
    prayer.)
There is your son. Here is your mother. Jn. 19:26-27.
I am thirsty. Jn. 19:28.
It is finished. Jn. 19:30.

Note that of the above sayings the least authentic is the most popular, and
the most authentic the least popular.
Note dependence on Psalms.
Why did Luke change Mark's quotation?
Note three different traditions of last word on the cross.
Note progress of interpretation in the last word.
Note one saying in Mark and Matthew, but expanded tradition in the other two
Gospels.

143

APPENDIX IV

Famous Ascension Narratives

MOSES

Now when they had come to the mountain called Abarim, which is a very high mountain located opposite Jericho, and one which affords to those on it a view of the greatest part of the excellent land of Canaan, he dismissed the senate, and as he was going to embrace Eleazer and Joshua and was talking to them, suddenly a cloud stood over him and he disappeared into a certain valley.—Josephus, *Antiquities* IV. 325-326.

HERCULES

Hercules, when he had commanded Hyllus, who was his elder son by Deianeira, to marry Iole when he had grown to manhood, having arrived at Oeta, which is a mountain of Trachis, built a pyre, mounted it, and commanded him to set it on fire. He however was unwilling, and Poias, who was there caring for his flocks, lit it and received his bow as a present. While the fire was burning it is said that a cloud descended with thunder and carried him up to heaven.—Library of Apollodorus 2.7.7.

ELIJAH

And as they were going along conversing, suddenly a chariot of fire and horses of fire separated the two of them; and Elijah went up to heaven in a storm. As Elisha looked he was calling, "My father, my father! Israel's chariots and cavalry!" But he no longer saw him. Then he took hold of his own garments and tore them in two, and he picked up Elijah's robe that had fallen from him and returned and stood by the bank of the Jordan. Then he took Elijah's robe that had fallen from him and struck the water and said, "Where is the LORD, Elijah's God, even he?" And he struck the water and it divided right and left and Elisha went across.—2 Kings 2:11-14.

ROMULUS

After these immortal deeds had been performed and he was holding an assembly to review the army on that plain by Lake Capra, suddenly a violent thunderstorm arose which enveloped the king in so dense a cloud that he was no longer visible to the assembly; nor was Romulus ever on earth again. . . .

Proculus Julius, to quiet the people, reported that Romulus later descended from heaven and appeared to him at daybreak, prophesied the future glory of Rome and ascended again to heaven. —Livy 1.16

RAPHAEL

I am Raphael, one of the seven holy angels who bear the prayers of the saints and go into the presence of the glory of the holy one. And the two were disturbed and fell on their faces, because they were afraid. "Don't be afraid, you will have peace; bless God forever, because it was not by my grace, but by the will of your God, so bless him forever. I was appearing to you all the time and was not eating and drinking, but you were seeing a vision. And now confess to God, because I am going up to the one who sent me; and write all the things that have been accomplished in a book." And they rose up and did not see him. And they confessed his great and marvelous works to God, how an angel of the Lord had appeared to them.—*Tobit* 12:15-22.

JESUS

He led them as far as Bethany, and lifted up his hands and blessed them, and while he was blessing them he was separated from them.—Lk. 24:50-51.

After his passion he presented himself alive to them by many proofs over a period of forty days, appearing to them and speaking to them of the kingdom of God . . . "But you will receive power when the Holy Spirit comes upon you, and you will be my witnesses in Jerusalem and in all Judea and Samaria and to the end of the earth." And while he was saying these things and they were watching, he was taken away, and a cloud received him from their sight. And while they were watching him go up into heaven, suddenly two men stood near them in white garments and said, "Galileans, why are you standing looking into the sky? This Jesus who has been taken from you into the sky will come again in the same way in which you saw him going."—*Acts* 1:3, 8-11.

APPENDIX V

Luke's Central Portion

9:51-56	James and John would call down fire	
9:57-62	Three would-be disciples	Mt. 8:18-22
10:1-20	Mission of seventy (framework, connexions)	
10:2	Harvest plenteous	Mt. 9:37-38
10:3	As lambs among wolves	Mt. 10:16
10:4-12	Instructions for itinerant preachers	Mt. 10:9-15, Mk. 6:7-11
10:13-15	Woe to Chorazin and Bethsaida	Mt. 11:21-24
10:16	Who hears you hears me, etc.	Mt. 10:40, Jn. 13:20
10:17-20	Return of the seventy (framework)	
10:21-22	Thank you, father, hidden from wise	Mt. 11:25-27
10:23-24	Prophets and kings desired to see	Mt. 13:16-17
10:25-28	Two great commandments	Mt. 22:34-40, Mk. 12:28-34
10:29-37	Good Samaritan	
10:38-42	Mary chooses better part	
11:1-4	Our Father (Lord's prayer)	Mt. 6:9-13
11:5-8	Called out of bed	
11:9-13	Ask and it shall be given	Mt. 7:7-11
11:14-15	Casts out demons by Beelzebub	Mt. 12:22-24, Mk. 3:22
11:16-23	A house divided against itself	Mt. 12:25-30, Mk. 3:23-27
11:24-26	Foul spirit going thru deserts	Mt. 12:43-45
11:27-28	Incipient Mariolatry	
11:29-32	No sign but that of Jonah	Mt. 12:39-41, 16:4
11:33	Light not put under measure	Mt. 5:15, Mk. 4:21
11:34-36	The lamp of the body	Mt. 6:22-23
11:37-40	The outside of the dish	Mt. 23:25 f.
11:41	Give alms for what is within	
11:42	Tithe mint	Mt. 23:23
11:43	Pharisees love front seat	Mt. 23:6 f., Mk. 12:38 f.
11:44	Tombs unwittingly walked over	
11:45	Bible student remonstrating (framework)	

11:46	You load men with burdens	Mt. 23:4
11:47-52	Tombs of prophets	Mt. 23:29-36
11:53-54	Conclusion to last item	
12:1	Leaven of Pharisees	Mt. 16:6, Mk. 8:15
12:2-3	The hidden will be revealed	Mt. 10:26-27
12:4-5	Fear not those who kill the body	Mt. 10:28
12:6-7	The sparrows	Mt. 10:29-31
12:8-9	Whoever confesses me before men	Mt. 10:32-33
12:10	Blasphemy against the Spirit	Mt. 12:31-32, Mk. 3:28-30
12:11-12	Be guided by Spirit in trials	Mt. 10:19-20, Mk. 13:11
12:13-21	The rich fool	
12:22-31	Don't worry	Mt. 6:25-33
12:32	Don't be afraid, little flock!	
12:33	Purses that don't get old	
12:34	Where your treasure is	Mt. 6:21
12:35-38	Dressed and lamps lit	
12:39-40	If owner had known when thief . . .	Mt. 24:43-44
12:41	framework, Peter asks	
12:42-47	Who is the faithful manager?	Mt. 24:45-51
12:48	Beaten with few stripes	
12:49	How I wish it were kindled already	
12:50	How distressed I am till it is over	
12:51-53	Do you think I came to make peace?	Mt. 10:34-36
12:54-56	Weather and signs of the times	Mt. 16:2-3
12:57	Why not decide yourselves what's right?	
12:58-59	Lest he hale you to the judge	Mt. 5:25-26
13:1-5	Do you think they were the worst sinners?	
13:6-9	Gardener asks second chance for fig tree	
13:10-17	Stooped woman healed in synagogue on Sabbath	
13:18-19	Parable of mustard seed	Mt. 13:31-32, Mk. 4:30-32
13:20-21	Parable of yeast	Mt. 13:33
13:22	framework	
13:24	Enter by the narrow door	Mt. 7:13-14
13:25-30	After the door is shut	Mt. 25:11-12, 7:22-23
13:31	framework	
13:32-33	Go and say to that fox	
13:34-35	O Jerusalem, Jerusalem!	Mt. 23:37-39
14:1-2	Man with dropsy	
14:3-6	Sabbath healing	Mt. 12:10-11, Mk. 3:4
14:7-10	Choice of seats at wedding	
14:11	moral	Mt. 23:12
14:12-14	Invite poor instead	
14:15-24	All began to excuse themselves	Mt. 22:1-10
14:25	framework	
14:26	Loving family more than me	Mt. 10:37

14:27	Bear cross and follow me	Mt. 10:38
14:28-33	Counting cost	
14:34-35	Salt losing taste	Mt. 5:13, Mk. 9:50
15:1-2	framework	
15:3-7	The ninety-nine	Mt. 18:12-14
15:8-10	The lost coin	
15:11-32	The prodigal son	
16:1-12	The clever faithless manager	
16:13	Can't serve two masters	Mt. 6:24
16:14	framework	
16:15	God knows your hearts	
16:16	Men enter kingdom violently	Mt. 11:12
16:17	One tittle of Law	Mt. 5:18
16:18	Judgment of divorce	Mt. 5:32, Mk. 10:11-12
16:19-31	Rich man and Lazarus	
17:1	Inevitable that hindrances arise	Mt. 18:7
17:2	Causing little ones to offend	Mt. 18:6, Mk. 9:42
17:3	If brother sin, rebuke him	Mt. 18:15
17:4	Forgive brother seven times	Mt. 18:21-22
17:5	framework	
17:6	Faith as mustard seed	Mt. 17:20-21, Mk. 11:22-23
17:7-9	Slave gets master's supper first	
17:10	moral	
17:11	framework	
17:12-18	Ten lepers	
17:19	moral, your faith has saved you	Mt. 9:22, Mk. 5:34, 10:52
17:20-21	Kingdom of God is within you	
17:22-37	Second coming	Mt. 24, Mk. 13
18:1-8	Unjust judge and moral	
18:9-14	Pharisee and revenue officer praying	

Index

Abiathar, see Ahimelech
Acts, see Luke-Acts
adulteress, passage on, 25
Aeneid, 6th Book, 101, 102
affinities to Pastorals, 125
Ahaz, 11
Ahimelech, 76
Alexander the Great, 3
Alexandria, 3, 4
Alexandrinus, codex, 20, 23
anachronism, 66, 68, 99, 129
anecdotes, 7, 68, 69
angels
  hierarchy of, 57, 119
  in church, 46
  see also supernatural beings
Anointed, 5, 10, 11, 38
anointing, of Jesus, 71, 75
  sacrament, 134
anti-Docetism, 128-129
  see Docetism
anti-Jewish polemic, 65, 134
anti-Semitism, 5, 41, 42
Antoninus, Pius, 135
Apocalypse of Enoch, 101, 135
apocalypses, 101-114
  beginnings, 101
  messianic hope, 101
  nucleus, 3rd of New Test., 18
Apollos, 35
Apostolic Fathers, 20, 108-113, 122-123,
  127-131, 135-136
apostolic teaching, end of, 84, 95
apostolicity, 16, 19
appendix, New Test. to Septuagint, 3
Apphia, 58, 127

Aquila, 35
Aramaic, 3, 74, 106
  cult cry, 49
  Hebrew dialect (Aramaic), 84
  Jesus, language of, 26, 63
  Mark, words in Gospel, 64
  New Testament, words in, 26
  Peter, language of, 77
Archippus, 57, 58, 127
Aristarchus, 57
Aristion, 135
arrangement of parts of Bible, 1, 2
  of Paul's letters, 2
ascension narratives, 144-146
Assumption of Moses, 135
Athanasius, list of New Test. books, 19
Athenagoras, and Pastorals, 125
Athens, 34
Augustine of Hippo, 27
Augustus, 1st emperor, 107
authors of New Testament, 14-15

Babylon, for Rome, 121, 122
Bacon, B. W., 7, 96-97
Barnabas, 116, 121
  parallels to Pastorals, 125
Bartimaeus, 72
Bauer, Walter, der Palmesel, 65
Beelzebub, 69, 72
Bezae, codex, 23
Bèze, Théodore de, 23
Bibles, two oldest complete, 20
Calvin, 60
Catholic Church, 130
Catholic Epistles, 2, 18, 30, 119-121,
  131-136

151

central portion, Luke's, 84-85, 147-149
chapter divisions, 2
chief features of New Test., 5
Christian names, 53
Christianity, from Judaism, 60-61
Christology, Johannine, 55, 57, 93, 98
  patristic, 129
  Pauline, 12, 13, 31-32, 55, 57
  Synoptic, 71-75, 83, 87, 88
Cilicia, 33
classics, 3
classless society, 38, 45
Claudius expels Jews, 35
Clement, 58
Clement of Alexandria, apostolic
  teaching, end of, 84, 94
  Hebrews, 116; emperors, list
  of, 107; Revelation of Peter, 114
Clement of Rome, see First Clement
clergy, orders, 48, 109, 122, 125, 130
collecting books of New Test., 1, 17-20
collection for poor at Jerusalem, 37, 49
Colossians, 56-58
  date, 57
  place of writing, 57
colt of Palm Sunday, 65
communion, pagan, 47
  supernatural power of, 46-47
converts to Judaism and Christianity,
  4-5
copying books by hand, 21
Corinth, 34, 35, 37
Costas, Procope S., language of Shepherd, 109
creation, Christ acting agent in, 13, 55-
  56, 98
Crispus, 34
cross, sayings on, 143, App. III
cursing Jesus, 47
Cyprian, 27, 47

Damascus, 40
Danaids, 59
Daniel, 101
deification of Jesus, 12-14
  of pagan heroes, 12
Deissmann, 43
Demas, 57
Demetrius, 133
denominationalism, 45

devil, 44, 72, 73, 112, 119, 120, 121,
  125, 131, 133
devout, those who fear God, 5
Diatessaron, 95, 118
Didaché, parallels to Pastorals, 125
Dimnet, Ernest, 62
Dionysius, bishop of Corinth, 60
Diotrephes, 133
Dirces, 59
divorce and separation, 45
Docetism, 49, 76, 83, 87, 129, 132
doctrinal guidance, 66
Domitian, 60, 105-107, 122, 134
dream, Pilate's wife's, 80

Eclogue, Vergil, fourth, 102
ecstatic experience, 39-40
  speaking, 47
Egnatian Road, 34, 53
Eleusinian mysteries, 49
Elijah, ascension, 144-145
Enoch, book, 101
entertainment, Gospel motive, 67
eon, divine emanation, 56
Epaphras, 57
Epaphroditus, 55-56
Ephesians, 117-119
  affinities, 118
  author, 117
  date, 117-118
  language, 117-119
  Pauline ideas, 117
  popular sayings, 117
  Schaff, Philip, appreciation, 117
Ephesus, 18, 35, 58, 127
Ephraemi rescriptus, codex, 23
Erasmus, text of first printed Greek
  New Testament, 21
eschatological discourse, 71, 78
ethics, 53, 120, 132
  codes of, 66
  primacy of, 133
Euodia, 55-56
Eusebius, 20, 25, 60, 76-77, 84, 94, 108,
  114, 116, 127, 133, 135
exorcism, 37, 69, 70, 72, 73
exposure of infants, 108, 109
expurgated editions, 137-138
extreme unction, see anointing
Ezekiel, 101

152

feeding of multitudes, 70, 73, 74
figures, striking, in Ignatius, 130
First Clement, 122-123, 136
  author, 122
  considered Scripture, 20, 21
  date, 122
  encyclical, 123
  language, 123
  parallels to Pastorals, 125
  Phoenix, 123
  purpose, 122
  use of Septuagint, 123
First Corinthians, 44-49
  date, 49
first fruits, 48
First Peter, 119-122
  affinities: Ephesians, 120
  author, 121
  1 Clement, Shepherd, etc., 120-121
  date, 119-120
  language, 120
  persecution, 122
  popular sayings, 119
First Thessalonians, 41-43
  date, 41-43
  read in church, 42
  reader's note, 43
First Timothy, see Pastorals
Fourth Gospel, see John
freedom from Scripture, 38
Froben, John, Basel publisher of first
    printed Greek New Test., 21
funeral passage, 42

Gaius, 133
Galatia, 35, 40
Galatians, 37-41
  date, 40
Gallio, 34
  inscription, 43
George Hamartolos, 107
ghosts, see supernatural beings
Gnosticism, 56, 124
God fearing (those who fear God, de-
    vout), 5
Good News (Gospel), 48
Gospel Lesson, 1
Gospels, the Four, 18, 62-100
  appeal of, 28-29
Gospel of the Hebrews, 25
Gospel of Pseudo-Matthew, 65

Gospels and Psalms, 67
Gospels become Scripture, 128

Hadrian, 135
hampers, 73
harrowing of hell, 118, 121
haustafel, 57, 120-121, 126
Hebrew, 3
Hebrews, 115-117
  author, 116
  date, 116
  language, 115
  parallels to Pastorals, 125
  popular passage, 115
  title, 115
Hercules, ascension, 144
Hermas, ambitions, 109
  inconsistencies, 110
  troubles, 109, 124
  see Shepherd
Herod Agrippa I, 95
historical chart, 139-140
Holtzmann, 96
Holy Spirit, 129
household regulations, see haustafel
hymnody, 85-86
  early hymn in Pastorals, 126

Ignatius' letters, 127-131
  attitude toward martyrdom, 131
  expansion of collection, 131
  date, 127
  Matthean parallels, 128
Illyricum, 54
Immanuel, 11
incarnation, 29, 56, 57, 98
infancy narratives, 78, 85, 86
Interpretation of the Lord's Oracles,
  136
Irenaeus, 77, 90, 106, 107, 108, 135
Isaiah, 11
Issus, battle, 3

James, Epistle, 133-134, author, date,
  King James version, language
Jerome, 27, 98, 136
Jerusalem, destruction, 8, 77
Jesus, ascension, 145-146
  birth, 8
  career, 9
  crucifixion date, 8
  deification, see Christology

development of ideas about, 13 f.
historicity, 137
"Jews killed," 41
mother tongue, 26, 63
Jewish expansion in Mediterranean, 4
Johannine letters, 132-133
  authors, 133
  date, 133
  Papias quotes, 133
  popular quotations, 132
  similarity to Fourth Gospel, 132
John Baptist, 35-36
  demotion of, 65-66
  followers, 35-36
  in Luke, 86
John, Epistles, see Johannine letters
John, Gospel, 92-100
  anachronism, 99
  appendix, 97
  author, 28, 94-95
  contrasts, 93
  date, 95
  devotional power, 92
  fish, one-hundred and fifty-three, 98
  language, 97
  literary sources, 97
  Old Testament parallelism, 81-82
  popularity, 92
  purpose, 99
  structure, 96-98
  three-year ministry, 96
  threes, fondness for, 96-97
John, of Zebedee, 107
  death, 95
Josephus, 8, 36
Judas, 80, 89, 128, 136
Jude, Epistle, 135
  name, 135
  use of Old Testament, 135
  Second Peter, used by, 135
Julius Caesar, first emperor in one
  list, 107
Justin Martyr, Apology, 14, 47, 95, 107

King James Version, 24, 27, 58, 133
kingdom of heaven vs. kingdom of
  God, 82
kiss, ceremonial, 42
Kleist, James A., 75
Knox, John, 18, 58, 127

Laodiceans, 57, 58
lapsed, 111, 112
last supper, 46, 71, 89
Law of Moses, 4
length of books, 2
letters of alphabet as numerals, 106
letters of Ignatius, 127-131
letters read in worship, 17-18
Letters and Treatises, 115-136
Lightfoot, J. B., bishop, 131
liturgy, 4
Livy, 12, 145
Lord's Day, 129
Lord's Prayer, Luke's, 63
  Matthew's doxology, 25
love, primacy of, 39
  universal solvent, 48
loyalty to Rome, 60, 122
Luke, companion of Paul, 57
  author, 91-92
Luke-Acts, 84-92
  author, 88
  central portion of Gospel, 84-85, 147-
    149
  date, 89-90
  formulas, 91
  language, 86, 90-91
  Luke based on Mark, 84
  Paul's death, silence on, 89
  purpose of Acts, 92
  special features, 87
  structure of Acts, 90-91
  use of sources, 86
  women, prominence in Luke, 88
Luther, 60

Macedonia, 34
magic books, 37
Magnesia, 127
man of lawlessness, 43
manual labor, Paul's, 41
manuscripts of New Test., 21-25
maran atha, 49
Marcan passages omitted from Luke,
  86
Marcion's Bible, 19, 90, 95, 116, 125,
  128, 136
Mark, companion of Paul, 57, 121
Mark, Gospel, 69-78
  arrangement, 71
  author, 76, 77

154

Christology, 73
date, 77-78
healings with saliva, 75
illustrations of main points, 72-73
language, 75
lines of teaching, 71
main source of Gospels, 69
omissions in other Gospels, 73-76
outline, 69-71
marriage of clergy, 45
Martyrdom, 8, 59-60, 77, 122
encouragement toward, 66, 67
Matthew, Gospel, 78-84
author, 84
date and place of composition, 83
discourse sections, 78-79
infancy narratives, 80
language, 75, 82
Mark main source, 78
Pharisees, 82-83
poetic features, 80-81
popular passages, 80, 81, 84
prophecy, 81-82
special features, 79-83
Messiah, 5, 10-11
Micah, 11
miracles, motives for inclusion, 66
not related by eyewitnesses, 78
Mithraism, 47
monastic tendencies, 36, 41, 45, 124
Moses, ascension, 144
Assumption, 135
myths, pagan, 126

naive concepts, 15, 141-142
Nasser, 3
Neoplatonism, 56
Nero, 55, 60, 95, 105-107, 121, 122
Nestle-Aland, Greek New Test., 24
New Testament, earliest books, 30
authors, 14-17
dates of writing, 8, 16-17
influence of, 28
manuscripts, 21-25
modern study of, 28-29
most thoroughly investigated, 137
original language, 3, 26
nuclei of New Testament, 17-18
number 666, 106

Odyssey, eleventh book, 101
officers, church, see clergy

Old Latin Version, 23, 26, 27
Old Testament, attitudes toward, 124
status in second century, 124
in first century church, 4
Onesimus, 18, 57, 58, 127
oral gospel, 62-68
factors in, 62
Origen, his New Test. books, 20, 134
on Hebrews, 116
Ostian Way, 60
Our Father, see Lord's Prayer

pagan cults forbidden, 45, 47
Papias, 20, 135-136
date, 135
on Apocalypse, 107-108
on Mark, 76-77
on Matthew, 84
on John, 136
papyri, in Beatty library and University of Michigan library, 22
parables by the lake, 78
of talents, Matthew vs. Luke, 63
patriarchal authority, 45
Paul, 30-61
arrest and imprisonment, 37
authentic letters, 30
chronology of life, 32, 53, 54
citizenship, 60
companions, 33-34
conversion, 31
death, 8, 16, 54, 59, 60, 89, 122
essence of teaching, 38
imprisonments, Caesarean, 54
Ephesian, 57
Roman, 54
inconsistencies, 33, 38-39
Jewish origin, 31
"Journeys," missionary, 33-37
name, 30
plan, 32-33
shipwrecks, 54-55
Pastorals, 123-127
authors, 124, 125
date, 124, 125
literary parallels, 125-126
popular quotations, 126-127
use now, 124
Pelagia, St., 25
penance, sacrament, 111, 134
Pentateuch, 4

persecuting emperors, 105-107
Peter, companions, 121
  execution, 8, 59-60, 77, 121
  language, 121
  primacy of, 82
  Revelation of, see Revelation
  writings ascribed to, 113
Pharisees, in Matthew, 82-83
Philadelphia, 127
Philemon, 18, 58, 127
Philippi, 34
Phoenix, 123
Phrygia, 34
Pilate, dates, 8
Plato, Republic, 98
  Apology, 45-46
  Gorgias, 45
Pliny, Elder, 98
  Younger, 47
poetry, Hebrew, 65
Polycarp, 90, 94, 127
  letter to Philippians, 125
  Pastoral affinities, 125
Pompeii, Christians there, 60
portrait of Christ, primitive, 110
postresurrection appearances, 78-79,
  80, 83, 89, 96, 98
pre-existence, 55, 56, 57, 115
presbyter, 119, 121, 125
printing, first of Greek New Test., 21
Priscilla, 35
program of public worship, 1
prophecy, 11, 12, 81-82
prophets, major and minor, 2
proselytes, see converts
Protestantism, from Catholicism, 60
Proverbs, chapter 8, 98
Psalms in Gospels, 67
Psalter, revised Latin, 27
pseudonymity, 16, 137
puns, Euodia, 56
  Onesimus, 58
  Syntyche, 56

Q, meaning and derivation, 79
Quirinus, 12

Raphael, ascension, 145
rejected books, 20
relics, 36-37

Renan, angels, 46
  Matthew, 84
repentance, 111
resurrection, 48-49, 78
  appearances in Mark-Matthew, vs.
    Luke-John, 86, 98
Revelation of John, 102-108, 136
  action, 103-104
  art, 104
  author, 105, 108
  brightness, 103
  Byzantine atmosphere, 102-103
  chants, 102-103
  color, 103
  date, 105-108
  language, 103, 106, 107
  letters to seven churches, 105
  mosaic, 104
  Nero, 105-107
  Old Testament borrowings, 104-105
  Orthodox Church atmosphere, 102-
    104
  purpose, 105
  savagery, 104
  sevens, 105
Revelation of Peter, 113-114
  Clement of Alexandria commented
    on as Scripture, 114
  Eusebius rejected, 114
  Greek fragment, contents, 113-114
  manuscripts, 113
  use, Sozomen, 114
Romans, 52-55
  appendix, 53
  date, 53
  doctrine, 52-53
  place of writing, 53
Rome, attitudes toward, 41, 60, 104, 122
Romulus, ascension, 145

Sabbatarianism, 129
sacramentalism, 94, 130
Satan, see devil
Saul, 30
sayings on the cross, 143
Schaff, Philip, 117
scroll, convenient size, 67
second coming, expectation, 6
Second Corinthians, 50-52
  conciliatory letter, 51-52
  disconnectedness, 50

how many letters? 50
popular quotations, 52
severe letter, 50-51
Second Peter, 136, affinities, author, date, quoted by Theophilus of Antioch, quotes Jude
Second Thessalonians, 43-44
author, 44
purpose, 43
Second Timothy, see Pastorals
secret, Messianic, 75
separation and divorce, 45
Septuagint, Bible of the Early Church, 3-4
influence on Gospels, 64-65
Sermon on Mount, 78
sermons in Acts, 91
Shema, 76
Shepherd of Hermas, 108-113
allusions to New Test., 112
autobiography, 108, 109
character, 110-111
date, 109-110
inconsistency, 110
language, 109
manuscripts, 112-113
parallels to Pastorals, 125
special interests, 111-112
structure, 110
shipwrecks, Paul's, 51, 55
Sibylline Oracles, 101
Sinaiticus, codex, 20, 22
Smyrna, 127
Spain, Paul's plan, 33, 53, 59
Sophocles, 125
Sosthenes, 35
spiritual body, 49
sufferings, Paul's, 51
under Nero, 105-106
supernatural beings, 15, 39, 57, 104, 110, 116, 119
supernatural power of communion, 46-47
support of clergy, 45
Sylvanus, 121
symposium, 1
synagog, for church, 109, 133-134
Syntyche, 56
Syria, 33
Syriac, versions, Old, 23, 26

Tacitus, clubs at Pompeii, 60
Tarsus, 31
Tatian, 90, 95
Diatessaron, 118
Ephesians, 118
Tertullian, 27, 60
on Hebrews, 116
textual criticism, 21-25
Textus receptus, 24
Theologian, Holy, 13
Theophilus of Antioch, 95
quotes First Timothy as Scripture, 125
quotes Second Peter, 136
Thessalonica, 34
Timothy, companion of Paul, 58
Tischendorf, Constantine, 22
Titius Justus, 34
Titus, Epistle, see Pastorals
Torah, 4
traditions, of Jesus, 5-8
drift, 98, 99
Trajan, 106, 122, 127
Tralles, 127
translation, 24, 26-27
Troas, 34
Tychicus, 57
Tyrannus, 36

Unity, 130
Ussher, archbishop, Ignatian letters, 131

variant readings in Gospels, 24-25
Vatican, 60
Vaticanus, codex, 22f.
verse divisions, 2
Vergil, Aeneid, Book 6, 102
Fourth Eclogue, 102
Vespasian, 66, 75, 107
virgin birth, 11
visions, 31, 39, 40, 51
objectivity, reality, 15
Vulgate Bible, 27

Washingtoniensis, codex, 23
"we" sections, 30, 34, 54
wealth, dangers of, 87
in church, 134
Welsh revival, 29
widows, order of, 126, 130

Wisdom of Sirach, 98
Wisdom of Solomon, 98
women, silent in church, 45
    prominence in Luke, 88
work, must continue, 43-44

worship instructions, 47
writers, NT, characterization, 14 f.

Ximenez, Cardinal, polyglot Bible, 21

Zebedee, 28, 94, 95, 133, 136